The Old House

HOLIDAY and PARTY
COOKBOOK

The Old House
HOLIDAY and PARTY COOKBOOK
By Erma Biesel Dick

COWLES BOOK COMPANY, INC.
NEW YORK

Contents

Preface

THE OLD HOUSE RESTAURANT, where the recipes in this book have been concocted, stands at 432 South Fifth Street, opposite the Cathedral, in Louisville, Kentucky. Legend has it that Judge John Rowan, owner of Federal Hill ("My Old Kentucky Home," immortalized by Stephen Foster), built the house in the 1830's for his own residence, and that he died there in 1843. The mantel in the second-floor dining room is a duplicate of one at Federal Hill.

After Judge Rowan's death, his town house was purchased by a family named Canine. Three generations of Canines lived and practiced dentistry there. During their ownership, steam heat was installed in the house — the first in Louisville. When the house was being renovated to become the OLD HOUSE RESTAURANT, the original steam boiler was so large it had to be cut up with an acetylene torch before it could be removed. The hearth where Dr. Canine melted the gold he used for filling teeth is today a charming wood-burning fireplace that adds warmth and cheer to the room. The floor of the bar is made of hand-hewn slabs of Ohio River bed stone.

When electric lights were introduced in the East, Dr. Canine and his sons installed their own dynamos and terrified Louisville with the first electrically lighted house. The lights were so bright that the first time they were turned on the neighbors became alarmed and called the fire department, which came dashing in a horse-drawn engine to put out the fire.

In the early days, many famous visitors were lavishly wined and dined by the Rowans and Canines in turn. So it is fitting that the OLD HOUSE RESTAURANT, known for its fine cuisine and drinks, should preserve and occupy this historic landmark. Today visitors from all over the world dine at the OLD HOUSE and enjoy walking through the rooms to look at the antiques, pictures, and furnishings of the period in which the house was built. In the main dining room there is a small but outstanding collection of rare old whiskies, liquors, and wines.

Located in the small building next door to the restaurant is the OLD HOUSE EPICUREAN, a gourmet shop opened a few years ago in connection with the restaurant. There food fanciers can find herbs and spices, sauces and seasonings, and unusual bottled, canned, and packaged foods from all over the world, including a few specialties of the restaurant itself. Gourmets in search of ingredients mentioned in this book that are hard to find where they live can order from the EPICUREAN if they wish.

It is with great pride that I dedicate this book to my patrons, the wonderful people who have made the OLD HOUSE RESTAURANT the success it is.

Erma Biesel Dick

New Year's Day Dinner

NEW LEAF
FRESH PAGE
BLOODLESS MARY
PICK-ME-UP
EYE-OPENER

BLACK-EYED PEAS
STUFFED ROAST PORK
WILTED SALAD
STEWED TOMATOES AND CELERY

PUMPKIN PONES
FRUITED BREAD PUDDING
WITH HOT BRANDY SAUCE

❈ New Year's Day

This occasion should be a quiet one for reflection, a day to think over one's life and to plan for the coming year. Unfortunately, most of us use it to recover from the night before!

In any event, after the Yuletide and holiday celebrations, we are usually saturated with rich foods and drinks, and are ready for a nourishing and unelaborate dinner like this one.

New Leaf

Juice of ½ orange
Juice of ¼ lemon

4½ ounces grape juice
Club soda

Put shaved or crushed ice in tall glass and pour juices over it. Fill with soda and serve with a straw.

Fresh Page

Fill tall glass with ice and add 3 dashes angostura bitters. Fill glass ¾ full with cold double-strength coffee, and fill to the top with club soda. Stir and serve.

Bloodless Mary

4 ounces tomato juice	½ teaspoon sugar
Juice of ½ lemon	Salt and pepper to taste
1 teaspoon Worcestershire sauce	Dash of celery salt

Shake vigorously. Strain into Old-Fashioned glass over ice cube.

Pick-Me-Up

½ jigger brandy	2 dashes maraschino
½ jigger dry vermouth	2 dashes Pernod
2 dashes curaçao	2 dashes orange bitters

Shake well with ice. Strain into cocktail glass. Add twist of lemon peel.

Eye-Opener

2/3 bourbon	Dash of Pernod
1/3 lemon juice	

Shake with ice and pour into cocktail glass.

Black-Eyed Peas

2 cups black-eyed peas	1 quart water
½ pound salt pork	1 chopped onion
1 slice red pepper (hot)	Salt and pepper to taste

Soak black-eyed peas overnight. Drain next day. Wash salt pork. Put in an iron pot or heavy metal pot with a tight cover. Add all ingredients except salt. Cover pot and let come to a boil, then reduce heat and let peas simmer until tender (about 2 hours). Add salt to taste. *(Makes 6 servings.)*

Stuffed Roast Pork

5-pound pork shoulder (picnic ham)

8 prunes

3 or 4 tart apples

2 ounces (4 tablespoons) butter or margarine

1 cup bread crumbs

½ lemon rind, grated

½ teaspoon brown sugar

¼ teaspoon cinnamon

Salt and pepper to taste

Have picnic shoulder boned and sew or skewer on three sides, leaving one side open for stuffing. Pit prunes. Pare and cut apples in small wedges. Melt butter or margarine and add crumbs, prunes, and apples. Add lemon rind, brown sugar, and cinnamon. Mix well. Season pork inside with salt and pepper and fill cavity with stuffing. Season pork on outside with salt and pepper. Place on rack in an open pan. Roast at 350 degrees, allowing about 40 minutes per pound. *(Makes 6 servings.)*

Wilted Salad

4 slices bacon

1 bunch spring onions, chopped with green tops

½ cup vinegar

½ teaspoon salt

1 tablespoon sugar

1 head lettuce, shredded

1 cup endive, shredded

1 cup fresh tender spinach leaves, shredded

1 hard-cooked egg, sliced

Dice bacon and cook until crisp. Add chopped onion and cook until onion is soft but not browned. Add vinegar, salt, and sugar and bring to a boil. Pour over shredded greens and garnish with egg slices. *(Serves six).*

Stewed Tomatoes and Celery

4 cups fresh tomatoes

2 cups diced celery

1 teaspoon salt

¼ teaspoon freshly ground black pepper

2 tablespoons butter

1 green pepper, chopped

½ teaspoon sweet basil

Place all ingredients in covered saucepan and cook over low heat until celery is tender. Keep pan covered while cooking to eliminate having to add water. *(Makes 6 servings.)*

Pumpkin Pones

2 cups cornmeal
2 cups mashed cooked pumpkin
1 teaspoon salt
2 tablespoons melted butter

Mix all ingredients well. Form into small pones and flatten slightly. Place on greased baking sheet and bake for 20 minutes in a preheated 425-degree oven. Serve very hot with butter *(Makes about 12 small pones.)*

Fruited Bread Pudding

2 cups bread cubes
3 tablespoons butter
½ cup hot milk
2 tart apples, diced
¼ cup chopped candied orange peel
½ cup seedless white raisins
½ cup chopped candied cherries
½ cup sugar
Grated rind of 1 lemon
3 egg yolks, beaten
3 egg whites, stiffly beaten

Saute bread cubes in butter and add hot milk. Mix lightly. Add apples, orange peel, raisins, cherries, and sugar and mix together. Add lemon rind. Add beaten egg yolks and fold in stiffly beaten egg whites. Butter baking dish and fill with pudding mixture. Set baking dish in a pan of hot water and bake for 45 minutes at 350 degrees. Serve either hot or cold with Hot Brandy Sauce. *(Makes 6 servings.)*

Hot Brandy Sauce

1 cup sugar
1 tablespoon minute tapioca
¼ teaspoon salt
1½ cups boiling water
1 egg
1½ tablespoons butter
¼ cup brandy

In top of double boiler, combine all ingredients except butter and brandy, stirring constantly. Cook sauce over hot water for 5 minutes until slightly thickened. Remove from heat and stir in butter and brandy.

Groundhog Day Dinner
February 2

GROUNDHOG FIZZ
SPRING-FEELING COCKTAIL

ROAST GROUNDHOG
WITH SAGE STUFFING
MOCK ROAST GROUNDHOG
WITH HERB STUFFING
SPICY BAKED SWEET POTATOES
WINTER TOMATO SALAD
WITH GREEN MAYONNAISE

ORANGE COTTAGE CHEESE PIE

❋ *Groundhog Day*

From the southern United States to the Arctic Circle lives the squirrel's chunky cousin, the groundhog or woodchuck. The groundhog grows more than two feet long and weighs from eight to twelve pounds. He digs his burrow in a hillside, ten or even twenty-five feet deep, with a nesting chamber at the end. Here the female gives birth to four to five roly-poly cubs each May or June.

From spring to fall, the groundhog nibbles clover, grass, roots, vegetables, and grain. In October he crawls into his burrow and sleeps until March, living on stored-up fat. Legend says that the groundhog comes out of his burrow every February 2, or Candlemas Day, to check on the weather. If it is a sunny day and he sees his shadow, he returns to his burrow for another six weeks of winter sleep. If it is a cloudy day, he remains out, and spring is just around the corner.

Groundhogs are considered quite a delicacy by some people, and are hunted throughout the summer. They are dressed and roasted whole like suckling pigs.

Groundhog Fizz

White of 1 egg
Juice of ½ lemon
1 teaspoon confectioners' sugar

2 ounces applejack
Club soda

Shake all but soda with cracked ice, strain into 8-ounce highball glass, and fill glass with soda.

Spring-Feeling Cocktail

½ ounce lemon juice
½ ounce green chartreuse

1 ounce dry gin

Shake with cracked ice and strain into cocktail glass.

Roast Groundhog

Clean and dress a young tender groundhog in the same manner as you would a rabbit or hare. Be sure to remove the white musclelike sacs that are under the front legs and at the small of the back. Soak groundhog overnight in salted water.

Drain the groundhog and place in a kettle in water to cover. Add ½ cup red wine and 1 tablespoon baking soda. Boil 1 hour, or until meat is tender. Remove from water and drain well.

Dredge meat with salt and pepper. Fill cavity with Sage Stuffing and skewer cavity closed. Sear meat on all sides in bacon fat in a roasting pan. Add 2 cloves garlic, 2 large sliced onions, 3 tablespoons each chopped parsley, carrots, and celery. Also add 1 teaspoon thyme, 2 teaspoons black pepper, and 1 teaspoon ground cloves, plus salt to taste. Baste meat with red wine. Roast, basting frequently, at 350 degrees for 1 hour, or until meat is tender and pulls away from the bones.

Sage Stuffing

½ cup white wine
4 cups bread crumbs
½ cup melted butter
½ teaspoon freshly ground
 black pepper

1 teaspoon salt
2 teaspoons ground sage
2 tablespoons chopped onions
1 tablespoon chopped parsley

Combine all ingredients, moisten with a little hot water, and mix well.

Mock Roast Groundhog

If you cannot find a real groundhog, this will taste just as good! Have the butcher bone a fresh pork shoulder weighing 5 or 6 pounds and make a large cavity in it for stuffing. Rub meat inside and out generously with salt and pepper.

Place meat in a bowl or pan and cover with port wine. Let meat marinate in the port for at least 8 hours. Remove and fill with Sage Stuffing or with Herb Stuffing. Roast meat in a very hot oven (450 degrees) for 30 minutes, turning it until browned on all sides. Reduce heat to 350 degrees and continue roasting, allowing 30 minutes per pound. Baste from time to time with marinade. *(Makes 6 to 8 servings.)*

Herb Stuffing

⅓ cup butter
½ cup chopped onions
¼ cup chopped celery
¼ cup chopped parsley
1 clove garlic, mashed

2 cups bread crumbs
½ teaspoon ground sage
½ teaspoon thyme
½ teaspoon tarragon

Combine all ingredients and mix well.

Spicy Baked Sweet Potatoes

Boil 4 large sweet potatoes in their jackets until soft. Remove skins when cool enough to handle and slice potatoes into a baking dish. Pour the following sauce over potatoes and bake at 400 degrees until sauce bubbles. *(Makes 6 servings.)*

SAUCE:

4 tablespoons chopped or
minced onions
1 tablespoon Worcestershire
sauce
2 tablespoons brown sugar

½ teaspoon paprika
½ cup water
½ cup wine vinegar
2 tablespoons ketchup
1 tablespoon poppy seeds

Mix all ingredients and simmer 5 minutes. Pour over sweet potatoes.

Winter Tomato Salad

1 cup V-8 juice
1 cup canned tomatoes, coarsely chopped
3-ounce package cream cheese
2/3 cup mayonnaise

3-ounce package lemon gelatin
1 cup diced celery
1 small green pepper, chopped
2 tablespoons chopped onion

Bring V-8 juice and tomatoes to a boil; add cream cheese, mayonnaise, and gelatin. Mix, cool, then add celery, green pepper, and onion. Pour into individual molds. When thoroughly chilled and set, unmold and serve with a blob of green mayonnaise on top. *(Makes 6 servings.)*

Green Mayonnaise

1 egg
½ teaspoon dry mustard
½ teaspoon salt
2 tablespoons vinegar
1 cup peanut oil

1 teaspoon garlic juice
1 tablespoon chopped dill
4 green onions with tops, finely minced
2 tablespoons chopped parsley

Break egg into blender container or mixer bowl; add mustard, salt, and vinegar. Add ¼ cup oil. Using blender at low speed or mixer at high speed, immediately pour in rest of peanut oil steadily. Add remaining ingredients and mix a few seconds.

Orange Cottage Cheese Pie

2 cups sifted flour
½ teaspoon salt sifted with flour
2/3 cup butter or margarine
2 tablespoons dry sherry
1½ pounds cottage cheese

1 cup very thick orange marmalade
4 eggs
Confectioners' sugar

Cream flour, salt, and butter. Add sherry and mix lightly. Add a little more sherry if necessary and mix until dough holds together and no longer sticks to sides of bowl. Roll dough out to line a generously buttered 10-inch pie pan. Cut remaining pastry into strips for lattice on top of pie.

Rub cottage cheese through a fine sieve and combine it with orange marmalade. Beat eggs until creamy, and stir into cheese-marmalade mixture. Beat until well mixed. Pour filling into pastry shell and place strips across top in lattice fashion, pinching edges and ends firmly together. Bake at 400 degrees for about 45 minutes, or until filling is firm and pastry is golden brown. Cool and sprinkle with confectioners' sugar just before serving. *(Makes 6 servings.)*

Mardi Gras Dinner

SAZERAC COCKTAIL

THE FAMOUS RAMOS GIN FIZZ

JAMBALAYA CREOLE

CAJUN BAKED YAMS
WITH CHUTNEY BUTTER

IBERVILLE AVOCADO SALAD

CREOLE PECAN PRALINES

CREOLE COCONUT CAKES

PLANTATION DEEP-DISH TOMATO PIE

CAFE BRULOT A LA OLD HOUSE

❋ *Mardi Gras*

The festival of Mardi Gras (literally, Fat Tuesday, a French term for Shrove Tuesday) has been celebrated in New Orleans since the days of the first French colonists. One legend attributes the custom to the French Canadian explorer Iberville, who founded the province of Louisiana in 1699. The cities of Biloxi and Mobile, which were two of the colonies Iberville established, still celebrate Mardi Gras, but the New Orleans festivities are the best known. Carnival season begins on Twelfth Night, in January, and continues as one mad gay fling until Lent. Pageantry, parades, costumes, music, and dancing are the order of the day.

Old House never misses an opportunity to celebrate — so here is a Mardi Gras dinner, to be enjoyed in costume, with dancing on the side!

Sazerac Cocktail

Put ¼ teaspoon Pernod into well-chilled Old-Fashioned glass and revolve glass until it is entirely coated with Pernod. Add ½ lump or ½ teaspoon sugar, 2 dashes bitters, sufficient water to cover sugar, and muddle well. Add 2 ice cubes, 2 ounces bourbon whiskey, then stir well. Add lemon peel.

The Famous Ramos Gin Fizz

The original recipe as made by the first Ramos of Spanish origin years ago in his bar, now long out of existence. Ramos's was located on Gravier Street facing one side of the old St. Charles Hotel in New Orleans.

1 jigger gin	½ white of egg
3 dashes lime juice	3 dashes orange-flower water
3 dashes lemon juice	3 ounces milk or cream
1 tablespoon confectioners' sugar	Club soda

Shake all ingredients but soda well with ice. Add a dash of soda and serve in tall glass.

Jambalaya Creole

2 tablespoons butter	1½ quarts fish stock from poached filet of sole or whitefish
1 large onion, chopped (1 cup)	
2 bay leaves, crushed	
¼ teaspoon ground thyme	¾ cup uncooked rice
2 tablespoons chopped parsley	3 cups cleaned shelled raw shrimps
½ teaspoon black pepper	
1 tablespoon flour	1 pound smoked pork sausages, cut into cubes
5 large tomatoes, peeled and chopped, or 4 cups canned tomatoes	
	1 cup chopped green pepper
	2 tablespoons Worcestershire sauce
1 teaspoon salt, or more to taste	
1 teaspoon chili powder	Pinch of cloves
1½ pounds filet of sole or whitefish, poached	2 pinches of nutmeg
	1 clove garlic

Melt shortening in large skillet. Add flour, meat, and chopped peppers. Cook, stirring constantly, for 5 minutes. Combine with all remaining ingredients except rice in a large kettle or pot. Bring to a boil, add rice, cover, and simmer for 30 minutes, or until rice is tender. Stir occasionally. *(Makes 6 servings.)*

Cajun Baked Yams

Scrub large red sweet potatoes or yams, rub well with butter, wrap in foil, and bake until soft, about 1 hour. To serve, unwrap, split partly, and fill with Chutney Butter.

Chutney Butter

6 tablespoons butter
1 teaspoon Worcestershire
  sauce

2 teaspoons finely chopped
  Major Grey's chutney
2 teaspoons chili sauce

Cream all ingredients together. Chill before serving on hot yams.

Iberville Avocado Salad

Soak 2 envelopes gelatin in ¼ cup cold sauterne, then add 1 cup very hot sauterne and stir until gelatin is dissolved. Add 1 tablespoon lemon juice and stir until well blended. Chill mixture until slightly thickened.

In a bowl, mash enough peeled and sliced avocado to make 1 generous cup pulp. Stir in 1 tablespoon lemon juice, ½ cup heavy sour cream, and ½ cup mayonnaise. Season mixture to taste with salt and coarsely ground black pepper. Add slightly thickened gelatin and blend well. Pour into oiled ring mold or into 6 individual molds and chill until firm.

Unmold on a bed of greens. Serve with ½ cup mayonnaise blended with ½ cup sauterne and 2 tablespoons chopped chervil. *(Makes 6 servings.)*

Creole Pecan Pralines *(Prah-leens)*

1 pound pecan halves
  (1½ cups)
1 tablespoon melted butter

2 cups brown sugar, firmly
  packed
4 tablespoons water

Mix pecans with melted butter. Add sugar to water and bring to a boil. Cook till it forms a syrup. Add pecans, stir till mixture bubbles, and remove from heat. Butter a sheet of heavy wax paper. Take one tablespoon of the mixture at a time and place on buttered sheet, pressing it into a round ¼ inch thick and 4 inches in diameter. Work fast. Leave till hardened and left with a knife. Pralines should be light, crisp, and flaky. *(Makes about 24 pralines.)*

Creole Coconut Cakes

1 cup finely grated fresh or
  packaged coconut

½ cup granulated sugar
2 egg whites, stiffly beaten

Add coconut and sugar to egg whites and beat again until stiff. Butter a thick baking sheet and drop spoonfuls of the mixture on it. Bake in a slow oven (275 degrees) for 35 minutes or till cakes begin to brown. *(Makes 12 cakes.)*

Plantation Deep-Dish Tomato Pie

2½ pounds fully ripe tomatoes
or 6 cups canned tomatoes,
drained
¾ cup granulated sugar
¾ cup dark brown sugar

1 teaspoon cinnamon
1 tablespoon vanilla
½ cup butter
¾ cup water
Pastry for single 8-inch pie crust

Combine pie ingredients in a saucepan and simmer 25 minutes. Meanwhile, roll out pastry dough very thin. Cut dough in half. Cut one-half into squares ½ inch wide. Drop dough squares into simmering tomato mixture and cook for 5 or 10 minutes. Pour tomato-dough-square mixture into a buttered baking dish. Cover with remaining dough. Prick top to allow steam to escape and sprinkle top with a little brown sugar. Bake at 450 degrees 15 minutes, or until crust is flaky and brown. *(Makes 6 servings.)*

Café Brûlot à la Old House

A chafing dish may be substituted for a brûlot bowl.

1½ cups brandy
Peel of 1 lemon and 1 small
orange, each cut in a thin
spiral
4 teaspoons sugar

1 stick cinnamon about 2 inches
long
2 whole cloves
½ teaspoon vanilla
2 cups very strong coffee

Heat ingredients, all but coffee, in a brûlot bowl or chafing dish. Dip out a ladle of the hot spiced brandy and ignite it. While it is blazing, lower the ladle back into the brandy and ignite the whole bowlful. Dip up some of the blazing liquid high above the bowl and pour it back into the bowl again. Do this a couple of times.

Pour coffee into the flaming chafing dish or brûlot bowl and blend by dipping up the liquid and pouring it back again. When the blaze has burned itself out, serve the café in demitasse cups.

Prepare and serve Café Brûlot in a room with little or no light. When it is served at the Old House, a member of the staff turns out the dining-room lights just as the brandy in the brûlot bowl blazes up. The lights are switched on again when the coffee is poured into the bowl, extinguishing the beautiful blue flames. A showy and delicious climax to the dinner! *(Makes 6 to 8 demitasse cups.)*

Shrove Tuesday Dinner

TRADITIONAL SHROVE TUESDAY PANCAKES
RED CABBAGE SALAD
EXOTIC SHEPHERD'S LAMB STEW

APPLESAUCE COMPOTE

❉ *Shrove Tuesday*

It is a centuries-old English custom to make and eat pancakes on Shrove Tuesday, the last day of Mardi Gras before Lent begins on Ash Wednesday. For that reason the day is often called Pancake Tuesday.

Traditional Shrove Tuesday Pancakes

2 cups flour	**2 eggs, lightly beaten**
Pinch of salt	**2 cups milk**

Sift flour and salt together. Stir in eggs and milk. Batter should be thin. Beat until smooth. Pour batter on a hot, well-greased griddle to make very thin cakes about 4 inches in diameter. Bake until brown on underside. Turn and brown on other side. Serve hot, topped with Exotic Shepherd's Lamb Stew. *(Makes 6 servings.)*

Red Cabbage Salad

5 strips bacon	**1 teaspoon dry mustard**
1 tablespoon wine vinegar	**1 small head red cabbage,**
1 tablespoon lemon juice	**shredded very fine**
1 teaspoon salt	**2 cups torn endive**
1 tablespoon sugar	**1 teaspoon chopped parsley**
¼ teaspoon coarsely ground	**1 teaspoon tarragon**
black pepper	**1 teaspoon chervil**

Fry bacon until crisp, remove from pan, drain, and crumble. To bacon fat in skillet, add vinegar, lemon juice, salt, sugar, pepper, and mustard. Bring to a boil, then pour over cabbage and endive. Add bacon, parsley, tarragon, and chervil. Toss well and serve while hot. *(Makes 6 servings.)*

Exotic Shepherd's Lamb Stew

1½ pounds boneless lamb neck, breast, or leg
1 large onion, chopped (1 cup)
1 tablespoon butter or bacon drippings
1 tablespoon flour
¼ teaspoon cinnamon
1 teaspoon salt
¼ teaspoon black pepper

1 cup orange-flower water
1 teaspoon sugar
4 tablespoons prune pulp (baby food is fine)
1 cup large potato cubes
1 cup carrots, scraped and cut into rounds
1 cup celery cut in 1-inch pieces

Cut meat into 2-inch cubes. Fry onion in fat until soft but not browned. Remove onion and brown meat in hot fat. Add flour, cinnamon, salt, and pepper. Stir and cook for 2 minutes. Add orange-flower water and sugar, and cook and stir until gravy is smooth but not too thick. Stir in prune pulp. Put meat cubes and rest of ingredients into a greased casserole and pour the gravy over it. Cover and simmer for 2 hours. *(Makes 6 servings.)*

Applesauce Compote

3½ cups sweetened applesauce
1 egg, beaten
½ cup milk
1 teaspoon cinnamon

1 teaspoon nutmeg
¼ teaspoon ground cloves
1 cup blanched slivered almonds
1 cup coconut macaroon crumbs

Mix applesauce, egg, and milk with cinnamon, nutmeg, and cloves. Stir in almonds and macaroon crumbs. Pour into a buttered baking dish and bake at 400 degrees for 30 minutes, or until a knife inserted comes out clean and the custard is set. Serve with whipped cream. *(Makes 6 servings.)*

Ash Wednesday Supper

PINEAPPLE MINT PUNCH
VERMONT FLUFF

TURTLE BEAN SOUP
LENTEN BAKE
SPINACH SALAD
CHEESE TOAST

COFFEE CUSTARD TARTS

Pineapple Mint Punch

3 cups cold milk	**1½ teaspoons lemon juice**
2 cups cold pineapple juice	**Dash of salt**
¾ cup cream	**12 drops peppermint extract**
¼ cup sugar	**Fresh mint**

Combine all ingredients except mint and shake or beat until foamy. Pour into tall glasses and garnish with sprigs of mint. *(Makes 6 servings.)*

Vermont Fluff

2 eggs, separated	**1½ cups milk**
½ cup maple syrup	

Beat egg yolks and 1 white. Add ¼ cup syrup and all the milk. Chill. Boil remaining syrup 3 minutes; pour over remaining stiffly beaten white; beat until cool and use as topping on beverage when served. *(Serves two.)*

Turtle Bean Soup

This can be made with 4 cans undiluted concentrated black bean soup, or with 2 cups dried black beans, cooked to a puree. To make puree: Soak black beans overnight. Drain and put them into 3 quarts water, with beef bones and a small piece of lean salt pork. Boil 3 hours, then mash beans and put through a sieve.

To make turtle soup:

3 pounds turtle meat	3 whole cloves
1 cup butter	1 bay leaf
3 onions, chopped (2 cups)	3 quarts beef bouillon
2 cups grated carrots	1 cup dry sherry
½ teaspoon thyme	Salt and pepper to taste
½ teaspoon marjoram	

Brown turtle meat in butter. Add vegetables and spices. Stir and cook a few minutes. Pour into a kettle and add beef bouillon. Cover and simmer slowly until meat falls from bones. Remove bones.

Stir in pureed black beans. The soup should be thick. Correct seasoning to taste with salt and pepper. When soup is very hot, stir in sherry. Serve with chopped hard-boiled eggs sprinkled on top and a slice of lemon on the side. *(Makes 6 servings.)*

Lenten Bake

2 12-ounce packages frozen perch or sole filets	½ cup chili sauce
6 medium potatoes	¼ cup salad oil
2 medium onions, finely chopped	1 teaspoon salt
1 small green pepper, chopped	⅛ teaspoon coarsely ground black pepper
1½ cups tomato juice	¼ teaspoon thyme
	¼ teaspoon marjoram

Thaw fish filets. Pare and thinly slice potatoes and crisp them in cold water. Heat oven to 375 degrees. Mix remaining ingredients. Place alternate layers of fish, drained potato slices, and tomato mixture in 2½-quart casserole. Cover and bake 40 minutes. Remove cover and continue to bake until potatoes are tender and browned on top. *(Makes 6 servings.)*

Spinach Salad

1 onion, grated
3 pounds spinach, washed,
  drained, and chopped finely
2 hard-cooked eggs, chopped
Mayonnaise

Salt and pepper
2 tomatoes, cut in wedges
Lemon juice
Chopped fresh parsley
Paprika

Mix onion, spinach, and chopped eggs with enough mayonnaise to hold them together. Season with salt and pepper. Form mounds on salad plates and garnish with tomato wedges dipped in lemon juice and then in chopped parsley and paprika. *(Makes 6 servings.)*

Cheese Toast

1 egg yolk
1 teaspoon butter
Brown or black bread

1 tablespoon grated Parmesan
  cheese

Mix egg yolk and butter to a paste. Trim crusts from 2 or 3 slices brown or black bread (pumpernickel, rye, or whole wheat). Spread with paste, sprinkle with Parmesan, cut slices in half or in triangles, and toast under broiler or in hot oven until golden.

Coffee Custard Tarts

2 cups milk
1-inch piece of vanilla bean
4 whole eggs
½ cup sugar

½ cup strong coffee
6 tart shells
Bitter chocolate, grated

Scald milk with vanilla bean and let cool. Beat eggs with sugar until light and lemon-colored. Add milk and coffee, stirring constantly.

Make tart shells of a rich pastry. If you don't have tartlette tins, use muffin pans (some cooks like them even better because they are deeper). Pour in custard. Preheat oven to 450 degrees and bake tarts for 10 minutes, then lower heat to 350 and bake until a knife inserted comes out clean. Sprinkle tarts with grated bitter chocolate. *(Makes 6 tarts.)*

Abraham Lincoln's
Birthday Supper

SPLIT RAIL
REFORM COCKTAIL

OHIO RIVER TURTLE SOUP
THE CRUSTY COUNTRY LOAF

OPEN APPLE TART AFTER-THE-PIG

❋ Lincoln's Birthday

Mary Todd Lincoln originally hailed from Lexington, Kentucky. During the years that she was mistress of the White House, social life in Washington was subdued because of the Civil War, so little is known of her tastes and talents in the culinary field.

A fitting meal for Lincoln's Birthday, however, would be simple and good, with honest homemade bread, unpretentious apple tart. You might start off by toasting the Railsplitter's memory, with a Split Rail cocktail.

Split Rail

1 ounce dry vermouth   1 ounce orange juice
1 ounce sweet vermouth   6 ounces dark rum

Fill a cocktail shaker half full of cracked ice. Pour in ingredients. Shake and strain into cocktail glasses. *(Makes 2 cocktails.)*

Reform Cocktail

¾ ounce dry vermouth   1 dash orange bitters
1½ ounces dry sherry

Stir well with cracked ice and strain into cocktail glasses. Serve with a cherry.

Ohio River Turtle Soup

4 pounds fresh turtle meat
4 quarts water
2 carrots, sliced in rounds
½ cup fresh green beans, broken
1 bunch celery with leaves, sliced in 1-inch pieces
3 large Bermuda onions, quartered
2 large potatoes, diced in large pieces
2 cups tomato puree, or 1 cup tomato paste
1 tablespoon allspice

1 cup green peas (fresh, frozen, or canned)
2 cups tomatoes, fresh or canned
½ cup ketchup
½ teaspoon Tabasco sauce
1 cup red wine (claret type, not too dry)
1 cup corn
2 cups shredded cabbage
1 lemon
3 hard-cooked eggs
Salt and pepper to taste

Put turtle meat and water into a soup kettle or pot with a tight-fitting lid and boil until meat falls apart. Add all ingredients except lemon and hard-cooked eggs. Cover and cook over low heat for 2 hours. Correct seasoning to taste. Serve in a tureen with paper-thin slices of lemon and chopped hard-cooked eggs floating on top. *(Makes 8 to 10 servings.)*

The Crusty Country Loaf

1 cup sweet milk, scalded
1½ cups water
1 cake yeast
1 teaspoon sugar

2 teaspoons salt
6 cups sifted flour
1 egg, beaten
Flake salt or sea salt

Combine scalded milk and water and cool to lukewarm. Add yeast, sugar, and salt to milk and water. Add flour gradually to make a stiff dough. Knead dough on a lightly floured surface until dough is smooth and elastic. Place in a greased bowl, cover, and put in a warm place till it rises double in bulk. Punch down and let rise again.

Knead well. Divide dough into two equal portions and shape into two long loaves about 2 inches thick. Sprinkle a board or pan with flour and place the loaves on the floured surface so that they do not touch. Again put loaves in warm place and let rise until double in size. Make diagonal cuts halfway through the tops of the loaves. The dough should spring back from the cuts or slashes.

Place loaves in a lightly greased pan and put in a preheated oven at 400 degrees for 15 minutes. Lower oven to 350 degrees and bake loaves 45 minutes longer or until they are crisp and well browned. Ten minutes before removing them, beat 1 egg with ½ cup water and brush loaves with this mixture. This will make a hard, brown, crisp crust. Sprinkle loaves with a little flake salt or sea salt.

Open Apple Tart After-the-Pig

Prepare pastry for single rich, flaky 9-inch pie crust. Crumble several pieces of crisp fried bacon.

FILLING:

2 cups thick, unsweetened
   applesauce
¼ teaspoon ground cloves
¼ teaspoon ground cinnamon
3 tablespoons melted butter

2 egg yolks, lightly beaten
1 cup brown sugar
Juice of 1 lemon
Rind of 1 lemon, grated
1 cup heavy cream

Line a pie plate with crust dough and sprinkle half the crumbled bacon over it.

Put the applesauce in a saucepan, add ground cloves and cinnamon, and stir in melted butter. Cool. Stir in egg yolks, sugar, lemon juice and rind. Stir in cream. Pour into pie shell and sprinkle remaining crumbled bacon over top.

Bake at 425 degrees for 10 minutes. Reduce heat to 350 degrees and bake 30 minutes. *(Makes 6 servings.)*

Saint Valentine's Day Supper

HEARTS AND FLOWERS COCKTAIL

CARROT HEART MOLDS
FRENCH VALENTINE PASTIES

LIQUEUR D'AMOUR

❀ Saint Valentine's Day

For centuries, February 14 has been observed as Saint Valentine's Day, though little is known of the saint himself. How it got to be the day for lovers may stem from the medieval belief that birds mated on this day. That notion apparently suggested the bygone European custom for young men and women to assemble on the eve of Valentine's Day and become sweethearts by drawing each other's names from an urn.

However you have selected your particular valentine, here is an appropriate sentimental supper to honor the day.

Hearts and Flowers Cocktail

½ ounce brandy
½ ounce dry vermouth
½ ounce grenadine
½ ounce orange juice
Dash of white crème de menthe

Shake with cracked ice and strain into cocktail glass.

Carrot Heart Molds

12 medium-size carrots
2 tablespoons grated onion
½ green pepper, chopped
2 tablespoons butter
1 tablespoon flour
1 tablespoon sugar
1 cup hot milk
3 eggs, well beaten
Bread crumbs
Crushed peanuts for garnish
Salt and pepper to taste

Cook carrots in salted water until they are tender. Drain and mash them. Saute onion and green pepper in butter until onion is golden. Stir in flour, sugar, salt, and pepper, then add milk and beaten eggs gradually, stirring constantly. Stir and cook until sauce is slightly thickened.

Combine this mixture with the mashed carrots. Butter individual heart-shaped molds heavily and fill with carrot mixture. Cover tops with bread crumbs, dot with butter, and bake 30 minutes at 350 degrees. Unmold while hot on serving platters with the Valentine Pasties. Garnish tops of carrot-pudding molds with crushed peanuts. *(Makes 4 saucer-size molds.)*

French Valentine Pasties

2 tablespoons bacon fat or drippings	1 cup cooked peas
2 tablespoons chopped onions	2 tablespoons Worcestershire sauce
2 tablespoons flour	1 clove garlic, finely chopped
1 cup dry sherry	1 teaspoon salt
2 cups cooked cubed meat, or cooked cubed chicken, or cooked flaked crabmeat	¼ teaspoon pepper
	¼ teaspoon thyme
½ cup cooked chopped mushrooms	Pastry for single 9-inch pie crust
	Pinch of powdered bay leaves

Melt bacon fat, add onions and garlic, and saute over medium heat until onions are soft but not browned. Add flour and mix well. Stir in sherry and stir constantly until mixture thickens. Add mushrooms and cubed meat (or cubed chicken or crabmeat). Add peas and seasonings. Mix well and keep hot.

Roll out dough for a flaky pie crust. Cut out two heart shapes the size of a saucer. Place one heart on a greased baking sheet. Spoon meat mixture into center of dough. Place another dough heart on top and, with a fork dipped in cold water, pinch edges of hearts together. Prick top of heart to allow steam to escape. Make a floral design.

Bake heart pasties in a preheated oven at 425 degrees until crust is well browned on top. *(Makes 4 saucer-size pasties.)*

Liqueur d'Amour

⅓ Pernod
⅓ kirschwasser
⅓ anisette

Serve in cordial glass, pouring one liqueur on top of the other.

George Washington's Birthday Dinner

WASHINGTON'S TODDY
COLONIAL COCKTAIL

CHESAPEAKE BAY OYSTERS
MOUNT VERNON PORK ROAST
WITH BRAISED VEGETABLES

WASHINGTON'S CHERRY LOGS
HATCHET ROLLS
TRIPLE CHERRY PIE
UNDER THE SNOW
SPICED SASSAFRAS TEA

Washington's Toddy

6 winesap or pippin apples
6 lumps sugar
1 pint light Jamaica rum
1 pint apple brandy
1 pint boiling water

Core apples. Put a lump of sugar in each apple and bake apples 20 minutes in 400-degree oven. When apples are baked, place in an earthenware crock and add rum, brandy, and boiling water. Keep crock close to an open fire, pouring the contents back and forth from time to time, taking care not to bruise or break the apples. The longer the crock stands before the fire, the better. Take care that the mixture does not boil. If you do not have an open fireplace, you can make this in your oven: Heat at 300 degrees for 45 minutes. *(Makes 6 cups.)*

Colonial Cocktail

A good toast, credited to Washington: "Cobweb breeches, a porcupine saddle, and a hard-riding horse to all the enemies of freedom!"

½ ounce grapefruit juice   1½ ounces dry gin
1 teaspoon maraschino

Shake with cracked ice and strain into cocktail glass. Serve with an olive.

Chesapeake Bay Oysters

¼ cup dry sherry
3 tablespoons flour
1 cup oyster liquor
¼ teaspoon salt
¼ teaspoon freshly ground
   black pepper

3 tablespoons butter
¼ teaspoon chopped fresh or
   dried tarragon
2 cups large oysters, drained
1 cup cream

Cream butter with flour. Add oyster liquor, salt, pepper, and tarragon. Cook over hot water or over a low heat, stirring constantly, until sauce is slightly thickened and creamy. Add oysters and cook a few minutes longer until sauce is thick and oysters are cooked, about 5 minutes. Take from heat and stir in cream and sherry. Serve over toast. *(Makes 6 servings.)*

Mount Vernon Pork Roast with Braised Vegetables

Have your butcher bone a 5-pound pork loin. Rub pork on all sides with a little vinegar and then on all sides with the following paste:

3 tablespoons Morton's coarse
   smoked curing salt
3 tablespoons coarsely ground
   black pepper

3 tablespoons honey
1 tablespoon rosemary
1 clove garlic mashed

Fill a roasting pan with 2 inches of water and lay pork in it. Roast at 350 degrees, allowing 25 minutes per pound. Turn the pork and baste several times. The meat should be well done in approximately 3½ hours, or a little longer.

After the pork has cooked an hour, place the following vegetables around it in pan juices:

6 small pared potatoes
6 small pared sweet potatoes or
   yams

6 medium whole peeled onions
6 small pared white turnips
6 small pared whole carrots

Pan juices should be reduced when roast is done so that vegetables are browned on top. Slice pork and serve remaining pan juices over slices. *(Makes 6 servings.)*

Washington's Cherry Logs

Cover straight sections of bananas with mayonnaise. Roll in chopped nuts and chopped maraschino cherries and place on a bed of watercress (or other greens). Garnish with red cherries with stems, and little hatchets cut from stiff colored paper or cardboard and fastened in slits in the "logs."

Hatchet Rolls

2 cakes yeast	1 tablespoon salt
¼ cup lukewarm water	6 cups sifted, enriched flour
1 cup milk	2 eggs, beaten
½ cup corn syrup, or ¼ cup honey or sugar	½ cup melted shortening

Soften yeast in lukewarm water. Scald milk, add syrup and salt; cool to lukewarm. Add 2 cups flour and beat well. Add yeast, eggs, and shortening; blend well. Add remaining flour to make a soft dough. Knead until smooth and satiny. Place in lightly greased bowl; grease top of dough. Cover well and put into refrigerator.

After no less than 12 hours or more than 4 days, remove dough and punch down. Divide into 2 parts. Roll out 1 part, and cut into strips 3 inches long and ½ inch wide, to make handles. Roll out remainder of dough and cut into hatchet-head shapes 1½ inches wide. Place one hatchet head at the end of each handle strip and pinch them together. Let rise in greased pans until double in bulk. Bake in a hot oven (425 degrees) about 20 minutes. *(Makes 12 to 16 rolls.)*

Triple Cherry Pie Under the Snow

1 cup canned drained pitted red cherries	3 tablespoons sugar
1 cup canned drained pitted Queen Anne or yellow cherries	⅛ teaspoon salt
1 cup canned drained pitted black bing cherries	1 cup kirsch or maraschino
3 tablespoons granulated tapioca	1 tablespoon butter, melted
	Rich pastry for single 9-inch pie crust

Mix all ingredients, stirring them thoroughly, and let stand for about 20 minutes. Line pie plate with pastry and pour filling in.

Preheat oven to 450 degrees. Bake pie for 10 minutes at 450, then reduce to 350 and bake 20 minutes longer. Remove from oven and cool completely. Top with Snow.

Snow

    1 cup whipping cream   **1 teaspoon kirsch or maraschino**
    ¼ cup sugar

Whip cream until stiff. Add sugar and liqueur, gradually beating until cream stands in peaks. Sprinkle ¾ teaspoon unflavored gelatin with 2 tablespoons kirsch or maraschino. Place over boiling water and stir until dissolved. Cool and add to whipped cream and beat a few minutes longer. Pile on top of cooled cherry pie and refrigerate until served.

Spiced Sassafras Tea

Put four 1-inch pieces of sassafras root with 1-inch stick cinnamon in a quart of water and bring to a boil. Boil for 5 minutes until tea is a rich red. While hot, add ½ teaspoon ground cloves, juice of 1 lemon, juice of 1 orange, and 4 tablespoons sugar or more to taste. Strain tea and serve boiling hot. *(Makes four 8-ounce glasses.)*

Saint Patrick's Day Dinner

IRISH JIG COCKTAIL
EMERALD ISLE COCKTAIL

MULLIGAN STEW
SAINT PATRICK'S MULLED CUCUMBERS
WITH DILLED MAYONNAISE

IRISH GRIDDLE SCONES

GRASSHOPPER PIE
IRISH COFFEE A LA OLD HOUSE

❋ Saint Patrick's Day

It has been said that there were no Christians in Ireland when Patrick began his work, and no pagans when he died. This is, of course, not strictly true, but he did manage to convert a good number of people. Many legends grew up in Ireland about him, the best known being the story of how he compelled the snakes to fling themselves into the sea. Saint Patrick's Day has been symbolized by the shamrock, the Irish clay pipe, and the "wearin' of the green." In New York, they used to paint a green stripe down Fifth Avenue!

Here's a dinner to gladden the heart of any Irishman — or just to celebrate the day itself.

Irish Jig Cocktail

2 dashes Pernod	**1 dash angostura bitters**
2 dashes curaçao	**1½ ounces Irish whiskey**

Stir in ice and strain into cocktail glass. Add olive and orange twist.

Emerald Isle Cocktail

1 teaspoon green crème de menthe

2 ounces dry gin
3 dashes bitters

Stir with cracked ice and strain into cocktail glass.

Mulligan Stew

3 pounds lamb leg cut in 3-inch pieces
2 very large potatoes, peeled and quartered
3 large tomatoes, peeled and sliced
3 large onions, sliced
1 teaspoon ground sage
1 teaspoon chopped fennel

1 teaspoon chopped dill
2 bay leaves
1 green pimiento, seeded and sliced
2 cloves garlic, chopped
Salt and pepper
1½ pints meat stock
4 tablespoons dry sherry

Put all ingredients but sherry in a large pot and simmer for 2½ hours. Just before serving, stir in sherry. *(Makes 6 servings.)*

Saint Patrick's Mulled Cucumbers

Pare, seed, and cut cucumbers into strips, enough for 4 cupfuls. Drop into 1½ cups boiling water. Add ½ teaspoon salt. Cook until nearly tender. Drain well. Chill and serve with Dilled Mayonnaise.

Dilled Mayonnaise

½ clove garlic, minced
1 tablespoon chopped dill
1 tablespoon chopped chives or green onions
1 egg

½ teaspoon salt
1 teaspoon dry mustard
2 tablespoons tarragon vinegar
1 cup salad oil

Put first 7 ingredients plus ¼ cup salad oil into blender or mixing bowl. Cover and turn motor on low speed (or beat slowly with hand beater). Immediately remove cover and add in a steady stream remaining ¾ cup salad oil. Turn off motor when last drop of oil has been added. Leave mayonnaise in blender and add:

1 clove garlic
2 anchovy fillets
4 green onions with tops,
    coarsely cut
1/4 cup chopped parsley

1 tablespoon lemon juice
1 tablespoon tarragon vinegar
1/4 tablespoon coarsely ground
    black pepper

Cover and blend on high speed (or beat hard with hand beater) for 10 seconds, or until vegetables are finely ground. *(Makes 1½ cups.)*

Irish Griddle Scones

4 cups flour
1 teaspoon salt
1 teaspoon sugar

1 teaspoon baking powder
2 cups milk

Sift dry ingredients together and gradually add milk to make a rather soft dough. Turn dough out on lightly floured board and knead gently for a few minutes. Cut dough into 6 rounds and then cut rounds into quarters. Bake triangles on a hot greased griddle until they are brown on the underside. Turn and brown on the other side. To serve, split, toast, and butter generously. *(Makes 24 scones.)*

Grasshopper Pie

24 large marshmallows
2/3 cup milk
1½ ounces white crème de
    cacao
1½ ounces green crème de
    menthe

1 cup whipped cream
2 cups crushed thin, crisp
    chocolate cookies
6 tablespoons melted butter

Melt marshmallows with milk in double boiler. Add crème de cacao and crème de menthe. Cool. Fold in whipped cream. Chill.

While marshmallows are cooling, make crust: Roll chocolate cookies until thoroughly crushed. Mix well with melted butter. Press into a 9-inch pie pan, spoon in the filling, and chill.

Irish Coffee à la Old House

Put 1½ ounces Irish whiskey and 1 teaspoon sugar in an Irish coffee glass or other heavy stemmed glass. Fill glass 2/3 full of hot coffee and top with whipped cream.

Purim = Feast of Lots

PUNCH FOR THE YOUNG
MOGEN DAVID SIPPAGE
STUFFED EGGS
CHICKEN LIVERS
PICKLED MUSHROOMS
SALMON AND CAVIAR ROLLS
DRIED BEEF ROLLS
AVOCADO SPREAD
TIPSY MOCK SCALLOPS
PALESTINE SOUP
COCK-IN-THE-POT
WITH POTATO DUMPLINGS
PRUNES AND BEETS
BUB

HAMAN'S EARS
KICHELACH
HOT TEA AND KIRSCH

❋ Purim

Purim is called Feast of Lots because Haman cast lots for a lucky day on which to slaughter his foes, the Jews. But due to the intervention of Esther with her husband, the king, the Jews were saved and Haman was punished instead. So Purim became a day of feasting and gladness, of gifts to relatives and to the poor.

"Bub" symbolizes the coarse meals Esther ate in the king's palace, where she refused heathen fare. Children with clappers and horns masquerade from house to house, singing and reciting comic verses. Parties, balls, and historic plays are characteristic entertainments, and the Biblical Book of Esther is read in the synagogues.

30

Punch for the Young

2½ cups orange juice
2 cups unsweetened pineapple
  juice
½ cup lemon juice

½ cup grenadine or more to
  taste
2 cups cold ginger ale

Combine juices and grenadine and chill. When ready to serve, pour over ice cubes. Add ginger ale and stir. *(Makes 10 to 12 punch cups.)*

Mogen David Sippage

4 ounces Mogen David Concord
  wine (a kosher specially
  sweetened wine, very heavy-
  bodied)

4 ounces or a little less of
  quinine water, according to
  taste
¼ lime

Squeeze lime and drop into wine. Stir all ingredients and serve unstrained. Delicious and very refreshing!

Stuffed Eggs

8 hard-cooked eggs
1 cup flaked canned tuna
½ cup minced celery
2 tablespoons minced green
  pepper

½ cup chopped almonds
1 teaspoon horseradish mustard
¼ teaspoon salt
Olive oil, enough to moisten

Cut eggs in half lengthwise. Remove yolks and mash. Mix with rest of ingredients and stuff lightly back into whites.

Chicken Livers

½ pound chicken livers
3 tablespoons soy sauce
1 tablespoon dry sherry

¼ teaspoon garlic juice
1 teaspoon horseradish mustard

Wash and cut livers in two. Combine all ingredients, pour over livers, and let marinate for several hours. Saute livers quickly and serve hot.

Pickled Mushrooms

1 pound fresh button
 mushrooms
1/8 teaspoon thyme
1/8 teaspoon coarsely ground
 black pepper
1/8 teaspoon fennel seed
1/2 teaspoon garlic powder or
 juice

1 teaspoon minced onion
3 tablespoons tarragon vinegar
2 tablespoons olive oil
1/4 teaspoon minced dried lemon
 peel
3 teaspoons A-1 sauce
1/2 teaspoon chopped parsley
1 small piece bay leaf

Wash mushrooms and trim off stalks. Mix all ingredients with mushrooms in a saucepan and cook over low heat until mushrooms are tender. Chill overnight.

Salmon and Caviar Rolls

Freeze a large slice of smoked salmon and cut while still frozen into paper-thin small slices. Spread with caviar and roll up. Chill.

Dried Beef Rolls

Spread thin slices of dried beef with sweet pickle relish and roll up. Fasten with toothpicks and chill.

Avocado Spread

1 cup mashed ripe avocado pulp
2 tablespoons lemon juice
4 tablespoons olive oil
1 clove garlic, mashed

1 tablespoon minced green
 onions with tops
1 teaspoon salt
1 teaspoon chopped dill

Mix and blend all ingredients until smooth. *(Makes about 1 pint.)*

Tipsy Mock Scallops

Cut halibut in 1/2-inch cubes to resemble scallops. Make 2 cups.

SAUCE:

1/2 cup mayonnaise
1 tablespoon chili sauce
2 teaspoons lemon juice
2 teaspoons finely minced
 onions

2 teaspoons chopped parsley
1 teaspoon salt
1/4 teaspoon coarsely ground
 black pepper
2 tablespoons brandy

Poach fish in own liquor with a little margarine, lemon juice, and salt. If there is not enough liquor, add enough white wine to cover the fish. Cook 15 or 20 minutes until done. Cool in liquid in which they were cooked. Drain and mix with sauce. Serve well chilled.

Palestine Soup

The Jerusalem artichoke is a native of eastern North America. Unlike the common artichoke, which is a flower head with petals, the Jerusalem artichoke is a plant with thick white tubers growing on the root like potatoes. It does have a flavor somewhat like the petaled artichoke but is prepared like a potato. It is easy to cultivate, thrives in the poorest of soil, and has an enormous yield. Because of its low carbohydrate content, it is excellent for diabetics and dieters. Jerusalem artichokes are best in the late spring and are obtainable at most fancy greengrocers.

2 pounds Jerusalem artichokes	Pinch of thyme
1 large onion	1 pint rich chicken bouillon
2 cups tomatoes	Chopped parsley
1 teaspoon salt	Chopped chives
¼ teaspoon pepper	

Wash and chop up artichokes. Peel and slice onion. Put artichokes and onion slices into a saucepan with just enough water to cover them, and cook until artichokes are soft. When done, mash artichokes and onion to a pulp. Add chopped tomatoes, salt, pepper, and thyme. Add chicken bouillon and mix well. Heat and serve with parsley and chives sprinkled on top. *(Makes 6 servings.)*

Cock-in-the-Pot with Potato Dumplings

4- to 5-pound stewing chicken	2 large onions, coarsely chopped
1 tablespoon salt	2 cups celery cut in 1-inch pieces
4 carrots cut in 1-inch pieces	4 tablespoons chopped parsley
1 small onion studded with	1 bay leaf
whole cloves	1 teaspoon thyme

Truss wings and legs of chicken close to body. Put in a deep kettle and add water to cover. Bring water to a boil and skim off fat. Add all other ingredients, cover pot, and cook slowly for 2 hours or until chicken is tender. When chicken is done, remove from pot and carve, and serve with hot vegetables and Potato Dumplings. *(Makes 6 servings.)*

Potato Dumplings

2 eggs
1½ teaspoons salt
2 tablespoons grated onion
⅓ cup potato flour

3 tablespoons matzo meal
4 cups grated raw potatoes, drained

Beat eggs, salt, and onion together. Stir in potato flour, matzo meal, and potatoes. Shape into 1-inch balls. Drop dumplings into the hot broth with Cock-in-the-Pot and cook until they rise to top. *(Makes 20 dumplings.)*

Prunes and Beets

1 pound unsweetened prunes
3 cups undrained julienne beets
½ teaspoon salt

4 tablespoons dark brown sugar
2 teaspoons lemon juice

Combine all ingredients in a stewpan, cover, and cook over low heat until prunes are tender.

Bub

2 cups very large lima beams
3 tablespoons margarine
3 tablespoons chopped onion

1½ cups cooked tomatoes
Salt and pepper to taste

Cook lima beans in boiling salted water to cover for 10 minutes; remove and drain well. Heat margarine in a saucepan and saute onions. Add the tomatoes, salt, and pepper and simmer 10 minutes. Add lima beans. Mix and pour into a casserole. Sprinkle generously with fine matzo crumbs and dot top with margarine. Bake at 375 degrees for 30 minutes, until topping is nicely browned.

Haman's Ears

2 eggs
3 tablespoons salad oil
1½ cups flour

1 tablespoon sugar
Oil for frying
Dark brown sugar

Beat eggs, stir in salad oil, flour, and sugar. Knead dough thoroughly. Divide it into 3 pieces and roll out very thin. Cut each piece into a round about 10 inches in diameter and divide into 4 sections. Leave for at least an hour. Fry quickly in a little very hot oil. Drain and sprinkle with dark brown sugar while hot. *(Makes 12 puffy ears.)*

Kichelach

3 eggs	¼ teaspoon salt
2 tablespoons cold water	2 tablespoons sugar
½ cup salad oil	4 tablespoons poppy seeds
1 cup sifted flour	

Beat eggs until light, then beat in the cold water, flour, salt, and sugar. Stir in poppy seeds. Drop by teaspoons on an oiled baking sheet and bake at 325 degrees until browned on the edges, about 15 minutes. *(Makes 3 dozen.)*

Hot Tea and Kirsch

2 ounces kirsch	Sugar to taste
2 ounces hot strong tea	

Put kirsch and tea in glass and fill with hot water. Add sugar. Twist a thin piece of lemon peel over the glass.

Easter Dinner

RASPBERRY LEMONADE
BANANA PUNCH
APPLE BLOW FIZZ

AN EASTER COCKATRICE

EASTER EGGS:
CANARY YELLOW
CARDINAL RED
PARROT GREEN

BUNNY SALADS
EASTER BISCUITS

EASTER LAMBS

Raspberry Lemonade

Juice of 2 lemons   1 ounce raspberry syrup
2 teaspoons confectioners' sugar

Put juice, sugar, and syrup in a 12-ounce glass with shaved ice. Add enough water to fill glass and stir well. Decorate with slices of orange and lemon, and a cherry. Serve with a straw.

Banana Punch

2 ounces vodka   Juice of ½ lemon
¼ ounce banana liqueur   Club soda

Pour into 12-ounce glass filled with crushed ice, adding soda last, and top with sprigs of mint.

Apple Blow Fizz

White of 1 egg   **2 ounces applejack**
Juice of ½ lemon   **Club soda**
1 teaspoon confectioners' sugar

Shake all ingredients but soda well with cracked ice and strain into 8-ounce highball glass. Fill with soda.

An Easter Cockatrice

Ask your butcher to save you the head, neck, and wings of a cock, leaving the feathers on and cutting the neck as long as possible. Rinse them in cold running water until all blood is drained and washed away. Dry and place in freezer to keep until needed.

Prepare the cock, or a whole stewing chicken, for cooking. Dress a domestic rabbit, removing the head and front legs completely. Cut off the tail end of the cock and press open the body just enough to allow the body of the rabbit to be pushed forward inside the body of the fowl.

Lay out 6 long strings on your work surface. Set the cock and rabbit flat on the strings, arranging the rabbit legs in a natural crouching position. Tie them securely in place. Pull the legs of the cock back over the body of the rabbit and tie firmly with string. When cock and rabbit are securely tied together, they form a creature that is half chicken and half rabbit. Put in a kettle and cover with water.

To the water, add 2 tablespoons salt, 1 teaspoon black pepper, 2 bay leaves, 1 teaspoon thyme, and a few fresh celery tops. Simmer gently until meat is quite tender but still tight on the bones. Take kettle from heat and let cockatrice cool in the water in which it was boiled. When cold, carefully lift out and drain well. Remove strings. Carefully separate fowl and rabbit.

Fill rabbit with the following stuffing:

3 cups fresh bread crumbs	2 tablespoons melted butter
1 tablespoon dehydrated minced onions	1 or 2 tablespoons water
	1 teaspoon sage
1 tablespoon dried parsley	¼ cup sesame seed
1 tablespoon poultry seasoning	1 egg, well beaten

Mix all ingredients well and cook over hot water for 15 minutes. Fill rabbit.

Carefully put fowl and rabbit together as before and skewer into correct shape. Pour a little melted butter over the cockatrice and roast at 400 degrees until well browned all over. Remove and cool. This show dish is to be served cold.

Set cockatrice on a nest of green parsley. Remove the cock's head, neck, and wings from freezer and skewer them in place, unfolding the wings of the cock straight back as far as possible, and arranging the feathers attractively. Arrange colored Easter eggs around the cockatrice on the green nest.

Easter Eggs

Peel 1 dozen cold hard-boiled eggs. Prepare as desired in the following manner:

Canary Yellow

1 cup pear vinegar or cider vinegar	½ teaspoon salt
	¼ teaspoon cracked or coarsely ground black pepper
½ teaspoon sugar	
½ teaspoon curry powder	⅛ teaspoon saffron
½ teaspoon garlic salt	

Let eggs marinate 2 hours. Eggs will be golden!

Cardinal Red

Put peeled hard-boiled eggs in a glass jar and cover with juice drained from canned sweet pickled beets. Do not pack eggs tightly in jar, but allow juice to cover them evenly. Stir or shake them from time to time, so that all eggs are thoroughly covered. Let eggs marinate for at least 2 hours or longer. Eggs will be a beautiful red.

Parrot Green

Use 2 tablespoons good heavy green crème de menthe to 6 tablespoons tarragon vinegar. Cover peeled hard-boiled eggs. Marinate 2 hours or more. Eggs will be a gorgeous emerald green.

Place colored eggs around Cockatrice. They look charming and, saturated with the various flavors, they taste delicious.

Bunny Salads

1 package lime gelatin	Lettuce
2 cups hot water	24 large whole almonds,
6 pear halves	blanched
4 tablespoons cottage cheese	Paprika
Soft pimiento cheese spread	Parsley
Mayonnaise	6 small cooked whole carrots
1 tablespoon chopped blanched almonds	

Dissolve gelatin in hot water. Pour into a pan 8x8x2 inches and chill until firm.

For each salad, fill pear half with cottage cheese mixed with pimiento cheese, mayonnaise, and chopped almonds. Invert pears on lettuce leaves on a bed of shredded lime gelatin made by forcing gelatin through a ricer. Make bunny's ears, mouth, and tail of almonds. Make eyes by dipping the pointed end of a knife into paprika. Garnish with small carrots, with a sprig of parsley stuck into the top of each carrot. *(Makes 6 servings.)*

Easter Biscuits

2 cups sifted flour	4 tablespoons cold shortening
3 teaspoons baking powder	¾ cup milk
½ teaspoon salt	

Sift dry ingredients together and cut in shortening. Add milk to make a soft dough. Place on floured board and knead lightly a few seconds, using as little flour as possible on board. Roll out ½ inch thick and cut with floured biscuit cutters or cookie cutters in chicken, rabbit, and lamb shapes. Place on greased baking sheet and bake in a very hot oven (450 degrees) for about 12 minutes. *(Makes approximately 12 biscuits.)*

Easter Lambs

Lightly rub a large lamb mold or individual lamb molds with a little melted butter. Press grated or shredded coconut against bottoms and sides of molds. Fill with softened vanilla ice cream and refreeze.

Remove from freezer when very hard, dip molds briefly in hot water, and invert on serving platter. With a little honey or melted ice cream, fasten a collar of crystallized violets around each lamb's neck. Pop quickly back into freezer until ready to serve.

April Fool's Day Dinner

SHANDYGAFF
FOOL'S FLIP
APRIL FIZZ

CABBAGE SOUP
PIG'S FEET ELEGANTE
BOILED SALTED POTATOES
KALE WITH EGGS

MIXED BEAN SALAD
DILLY ROLLS
WITH DILLED BUTTER

VINEGAR COBBLER

❋ *April Fool's Day Dinner*

Here is a fun dinner to serve to friends on April Fool's Day. It is a double joke, for all the dishes on the menu sound unappetizing — your guests will think you have certainly lost your mind! — but, in fact, every dish, no matter how dubious its name, is just delicious.

For full effect, play your joke to the hilt. Send formal invitations for dinner at eight, black tie. Set the table with all your silver, a splendid centerpiece, and plenty of candles. If possible, hire a butler for the evening. Fancy place cards and a menu at every place are a must.

When your formally attired guests sit down to your beautiful table and read that the *pièce de résistance* of the dinner is pig's feet, you will enjoy their startled reaction. But it will be even more fun to see their expressions change as they taste, and then to have a good laugh all around.

Shandygaff

Fill a large glass or mug half full of beer or ale, then fill the glass or mug to the top with ginger ale.

Fool's Flip

1 cup prune pulp (strained baby food is an easy out)   3 cups chilled milk

Beat milk into prune pulp with a rotary beater or shake in shaker. Pour into cocktail glasses. Top with a few gratings of lemon and orange rind.

April Fizz

¼ cup maple syrup   Ginger ale
1 quart chilled milk

Add maple syrup to milk and mix well. Pour into highball glasses and fill with ginger ale.

(This will be the most sober dinner party you have ever given!)

Cabbage Soup

1 pound lean beef   5 cups stock or water
½ pound fat pork, diced   1 bay leaf
1 large head white cabbage,   2 teaspoons salt
   shredded   ¼ teaspoon pepper
1 large tomato, quartered   ½ teaspoon savory
1 large onion, sliced   Sour cream

Combine meat and vegetables and add stock or water. Add seasonings and simmer slowly for several hours, or until meat is tender. Remove meat from soup, cut into slices, and serve a slice of meat in each soup plate. Garnish with a blob of sour cream in center of meat. *(Makes 6 servings.)*

Pig's Feet Elegante

6 pig's feet   1 stalk celery, chopped
1 clove garlic   2 carrots, diced
2 large onions, sliced   ½ teaspoon thyme
2 bay leaves   Water barely to cover
½ teaspoon coarsely ground   1 pound drained sauerkraut
   black pepper

Have butcher split pig's feet. Wash thoroughly. Put pig's feet into a kettle with rest of ingredients except sauerkraut. Cover kettle and cook slowly until pig's feet are tender. Do not add more water unless necessary to keep from scorching. When pig's feet are tender, add sauerkraut and heat thoroughly. Serve with Boiled Salted Potatoes. *(Makes 6 servings.)*

Boiled Salted Potatoes

6 medium-size potatoes
¼ cup melted butter (½ stick)
2 tablespoons minced chives,
   dried or fresh

1 teaspoon lemon juice
⅓ cup chopped parsley
1 tablespoon basil
2 tablespoons coarse salt

Pare potatoes and boil in plain water. When potatoes are done, drain, add rest of ingredients, and toss well. Serve immediately. *(Makes 6 servings.)*

Kale with Eggs

4 pounds kale
Boiling water
6 hard-boiled eggs, sliced
1 cup cream

1 tablespoon butter
¼ cup minced parsley
½ teaspoon chervil

Wash kale and remove stems. Place in kettle of boiling water to cover and cook uncovered about 30 minutes, or until tender. Drain. Put sliced eggs, cream, butter, parsley, and chervil in a double boiler and stir over medium heat until heated thoroughly. Do not let cream boil. Pour over kale and serve immediately. *(Makes 6 servings.)*

Mixed Bean Salad

½ cup French-cut green beans,
   cooked
½ cup wax beans cut into 1-inch
   pieces
½ cup drained canned
   butterbeans
½ cup drained canned red
   kidney beans

½ cup drained canned garbanzo
   beans or chick-peas
½ cup chopped pimiento
½ cup chopped sweet pickles
½ cup chopped celery
1 medium-size Bermuda onion,
   chopped

1 egg yolk
¼ cup lemon juice (or more for tartness)
⅔ cup condensed milk
¼ cup olive oil or salad oil

½ teaspoon salt
1 teaspoon dry mustard
¼ teaspoon freshly ground black pepper
¼ teaspoon marjoram

Prepare beans and other salad ingredients. Combine all dressing ingredients. Beat well until mixture thickens. *(Makes 1½ cups dressing.)* Add to mixed beans. Stir well and serve heaped in lettuce cups. *(Makes 6 servings.)*

Dilly Rolls

1 package dry yeast
¼ cup warm water
1 cup creamy cottage cheese
1 tablespoon dehydrated minced onion
1 tablespoon melted butter

1 teaspoon salt
¼ teaspoon baking soda
1 egg
2 tablespoons chopped dill
2¼ cups flour

Put yeast and warm water into blender or mixing bowl and let stand 5 minutes. Blend at high speed, or beat hard with hand beater, 20 seconds. Add rest of ingredients except flour. Cover and blend at high speed, or beat hard with hand beater, for 20 seconds.

Measure flour into a bowl. Pour blended mixture over flour and mix with spoon, adding if necessary about ½ cup more flour to make a stiff dough that pulls away from side of bowl. Pick up dough with floured hands and pat into a ball. Return to bowl, cover, and let rise until double in bulk.

Shape into tiny rolls, place in pan, cover, and let rise until double in size. Bake in a preheated oven at 350 degrees for 40 or 50 minutes. Serve with Dilled Butter. *(Makes 24 rolls.)*

Dilled Butter

Put 1 pound butter in a mixing bowl and leave at room temperature until soft. Add 4 tablespoons dill (chopped, fresh, or dried), 1 tablespoon onion juice, and stir until butter is thoroughly mixed with seasonings. Return butter to refrigerator to harden.

Vinegar Cobbler

2 tablespoons flour
2½ cups sugar
¼ pound (1 stick) butter
½ teaspoon cinnamon

½ teaspoon nutmeg
2 cups cold water
½ cup cider vinegar
1 teaspoon vanilla

DUMPLING DOUGH:

1 egg
1 cup vegetable shortening
Scant teaspoon salt

2½ cups flour
1 tablespoon vinegar
9 tablespoons ice water

Cream flour, sugar, butter, cinnamon, and nutmeg together. Mix water, vinegar, and vanilla. Combine and stir over hot water in double boiler until liquid is thoroughly mixed.

Make dumplings: Cream egg, shortening, salt, and flour. Add vinegar and water and mix dough. Roll out and cut into dumplings. Save enough dough for a thin crust over the cobbler.

Bring hot liquid mixture to a boil and drop dumplings into it. There should not be too many dumplings or the cobbler will be too dry (leave some dumplings out if the liquid begins to look overcrowded). Boil dumplings about 5 minutes. Pour liquid with dumplings into a baking dish; put a thin crust on top; sprinkle crust with sugar and dot with butter. Bake only until crust is browned. *(Makes 6 servings.)*

Income Tax Day Supper

BALM FOR THE TAXED SPIRIT
BUTTERMILK SOOTHER
GIN COMFORTER

TOMATO AND ONION PIE
POTTED PINTOS IN RED WINE
HAMBURGERS

DESTITUTION DESSERT

Balm for the Taxed Spirit

½ bottle champagne	1 tablespoon sugar
½ pint dry sherry	A few balm leaves
½ cup brandy	1 large bottle club soda
1 ounce noyeau	

Put champagne, sherry, brandy, noyeau, sugar, and balm leaves into pitcher. Stir and let stand for a few minutes, then add ice cubes and club soda. Serve at once.

Buttermilk Soother

1 ounce vodka	½ teaspoon salt
Pinch of black pepper, freshly ground	2 crushed cardamom seeds
	1 cup buttermilk

Pour vodka over ice cubes in 8-ounce highball glass. Add salt, pepper, and cardamom. Fill glass with fresh buttermilk and sprinkle a little pepper on top.

Gin Comforter

1 cup condensed tomato soup
1 cup condensed consommé
2 cups water
¼ teaspoon ground marjoram

¼ teaspoon ground thyme
1 tablespoon butter
Gin
1 lemon, sliced thin

Combine soups and water; add spices and butter. Simmer until all is mixed well. Pour into small pottery mugs. Add ½ ounce gin to each mug. Float thin lemon slice on top. *(Makes 6 servings.)*

Tomato and Onion Pie

3 large Bermuda onions
½ cup butter
3 large tomatoes

Salt and pepper
Bread crumbs
Finely chopped fresh parsley

Peel onions, cover with boiling water, and let them remain in the water until it is cold. Then drain and dry onions thoroughly, and cut them into slices. In a frying pan over low heat, saute the onion slices in butter until soft but not browned. Keep slices intact by lifting them with a broad spatula.

Slice tomatoes and place in alternate layers with onion slices in a buttered pie dish, sprinkling each layer lightly with salt, pepper, bread crumbs, and chopped parsley. Cover top layer, after the seasonings, liberally with bread crumbs, dot with butter, and bake in a hot oven (400 degrees) 30 minutes. *(Makes 6 servings.)*

Potted Pintos in Red Wine

2 cups dried pinto beans
6 slices raw bacon, coarsely
   chopped
2 tablespoons chopped onion
2 tablespoons butter
2 tablespoons flour

1 teaspoon salt
¼ teaspoon coarsely ground
   black pepper
1 teaspoon oregano
1 teaspoon rosemary
1 cup red wine

Soak beans overnight in water to cover. Simmer them in the soaking water with bacon and salt for 2 hours. Drain the beans and keep them hot.

Saute onion in butter 5 minutes. Add flour and seasonings and stir well until smooth. Add wine and cook until thickened, stirring constantly. Add beans and mix well. Pour into old-fashioned bean pot or widemouthed pottery jar and keep hot in oven until served. *(Makes 6 servings.)*

Hamburgers

2 pounds ground lean beef
  (round or chuck)
4 tablespoons minced parsley
4 tablespoons minced onion
4 tablespoons capers

2 teaspoons salt
1 teaspoon coarsely ground
  black pepper
2 teaspoons ground sage
2 teaspoons liquid smoke

Mix all ingredients thoroughly. Form meat into individual burgers 2 inches thick. Broil to desired doneness. *(Makes 6 servings.)*

Destitution Dessert

12 slices stale bread with crusts
  cut off
¾ cup honey

½ cup sugar
¼ pound butter (1 stick)
Whipped cream

Dice bread. Mix bread with honey, sugar, and butter over low heat, stirring constantly, until mixture becomes a moist paste. Press into a shallow round dish or pie plate. Chill in refrigerator until very cold. Cut into wedges like a pie and serve with whipped cream. (Or you can use a small loaf pan, cut chilled dessert into slices like cake, and serve with whipped cream.) *(Makes 6 servings.)*

Passover Supper

SOUP WITH MATZO KLOESE

POTATO STEAKS
STUFFED CORNISH HEN
PEAS AND KLOESE

HAROSETH
CHREMSEL
JACOB PUDDING

❋ *Passover*

The Jewish Passover is a celebration to commemorate the deliverance of the Israelites from Egypt.

It falls in the early spring, at about the same time as the Christian Easter. (The Last Supper of Christ and His Disciples was the opening feast of Passover.) Passover begins on the fourteenth day of the Jewish month of Nisan, and lasts till the twenty-first. This is a happy time of rejoicing, but the first and last days are kept as holy days.

On the eve of Passover, a festive board is prepared with the best linens, china, and silver. The menu is made up of ingredients symbolic of the ancient time when the Israelites were forced to leave Egypt in such a hurry that they had no time to let their bread rise but had to take unleavened dough with them and bake it on the way. A roasted lamb bone or a roasted egg commemorates the burnt offering the Hebrews were commanded to offer when God promised to pass over their houses and spare their firstborn. Horseradish or bitter herbs represent the bitter life of the Israelites in Egypt. A paste of nuts, apples, and spices, made to resemble clay or mortar used in building, is a sign of the heavy toil exacted by the Egyptians.

Soup with Matzo Kloese

SOUP:

1 quart soup stock	Potato flour
1 egg	Salt

Add a little salt and stir as much flour into egg as possible. Knead it well and roll it out as thin as a wafer. Divide it into 3 strips. Let these dry thoroughly, then shred finely. Bring stock to a boil. Drop in shredded strips and simmer 20 minutes. Skim off fat, add Matzo Kloese, and serve at once. *(Makes 6 servings.)*

MATZO KLOESE:

1 matzo	½ teaspoon ground ginger
1 onion, coarsely chopped	2 tablespoons matzo crumbs
2 tablespoons margarine	Salt and pepper
1 egg, well beaten	

Soften matzo in cold water and squeeze dry. Brown onion in margarine and stir into matzo. Add egg, ginger, and salt and pepper to taste. Stir in crumbs last and shape into balls. Roll balls lightly in matzo crumbs and drop them into soup when boiling. Boil gently for 20 minutes. *(Makes enough for 1 quart of soup.)*

Potato Steaks

6 medium potatoes, peeled, cooked, and mashed	½ teaspoon coarsely ground black pepper
2 eggs	2 tablespoons chicken fat, or more if needed
4 tablespoons potato flour	
½ teaspoon celery salt	

Drain all excess moisture from potatoes. Mix all ingredients except chicken fat. Heat fat in skillet and drop small portions of potato mixture, 2 or 3 tablespoons at at time, into hot melted fat. Cook over low heat until golden brown on both sides. *(Makes 6 servings.)*

Stuffed Cornish Hen

6 Cornish game hens, 12 to 14 ounces each	1 quart white stock

WHITE STOCK:

1 pound chicken wings	1 strip celery, diced
½ teaspoon salt	½ teaspoon minced parsley
1 quart water	¼ teaspoon thyme
1 carrot, shredded	1 bay leaf
1 onion, finely chopped	⅛ teaspoon black pepper
1 turnip, shredded	Pinch of ground cloves

Have butcher chop up chicken wings into small pieces. Put them into a kettle with salt and water and let stand for 1 hour. Bring to a boil and remove fat as it rises. When stock is clear, add rest of ingredients. Let stock boil up, then lower heat to simmer. Simmer 1 hour, skimming off fat as it rises.

While the stock is simmering, stuff the hens.

STUFFING:

1 large onion, chopped	1 cup matzo crumbs
2 tablespoons chicken fat	1 egg, well beaten
1 pound chicken livers, coarsely chopped	1 teaspoon chopped parsley
½ teaspoon salt	½ teaspoon salt
¼ teaspoon pepper	¼ teaspoon coarsely ground black pepper

Saute onion in melted chicken fat until golden. Add chicken livers and season to taste with salt and pepper. Saute livers until done and remove from heat. Add matzo crumbs, egg, parsley, salt, and pepper. Combine all and fill Cornish hens, sewing cavities tightly shut. Cook with brown rice.

RICE:

1 pound brown rice	Juice of large lemon
4 egg yokes, beaten	(2 tablespoons)

Wash and drain rice. Put into large kettle with unstrained stock and bring it to a boil. Cook slowly until rice begins to soften. Put hens in, covering them well with rice. Cover kettle tightly, and cook gently until hens are done, about 1 hour. Remove hens from rice and keep hot. To rice, add egg yolks and lemon juice. Stir over heat a few minutes, then serve piled around the hens. *(Makes 6 servings.)*

Peas and Kloese

2 10-ounce packages frozen peas
Sugar

Cook peas in just enough salted water to cover, with a little sugar added.
When peas are tender, drain nearly all the water off. Then make a pint of
batter as follows:

BATTER:

4 heaped tablespoons potato
  flour
2 eggs
½ teaspoon salt
1 pint rich chicken broth

2 tablespoons margarine
½ teaspoon chopped parsley
½ teaspoon ground ginger
¼ teaspoon pepper
Salt

Mix flour with eggs and salt, stirring until smooth. Add broth by degrees
until a thick, smooth batter is formed. Mix into batter the parsley, ginger,
pepper, and salt to taste, and mix well.

To the peas, with a tad of water left in them, add margarine and stir
well. Pour batter on peas in full tablespoons. Bring gently to boiling point,
then let simmer 30 minutes. *(Makes 6 servings.)*

Haroseth

2 large apples
½ cup honey
½ cup sultanas

½ cup almonds
Cinnamon

Peel and finely chop apples. Mix them with other ingredients and roll
into small balls.

Chremsel

2 matzos
1 cup fine matzo crumbs
2 eggs
½ cup ground almonds
¾ cup seedless raisins
½ cup sultanas

½ cup brown sugar, firmly
  packed
½ teaspoon cinnamon
¼ teaspoon ground nutmeg
Frying oil

Soak matzos in a little water and squeeze dry. Stir in half of matzo
crumbs and 1 egg. Beat remaining egg and add it to almonds, raisins, sultanas,
sugar, cinnamon, and nutmeg. Combine the two mixtures to make a paste.

Take up a little paste at a time. Smooth it carefully, roll it in remaining matzo crumbs, and fry in hot oil until nicely browned on all sides. Serve with a fruit syrup. *(Makes 6 servings.)*

Jacob Pudding

4 matzos	**2 eggs**
4 teaspoons margarine	**Salt**
½ cup orange marmalade	**2 cups orange juice**

Spread margarine and thick layer of marmalade on matzos. Break into fingers and place fingers lattice-fashion in a greased pie dish. Beat eggs well, add a pinch of salt and the orange juice. Stir well. Pour over jam fingers in pie dish. Let dish stand covered for 1 hour, then bake at 350 degrees for 30 to 40 minutes, or until a knife inserted into middle comes out clean. *(Makes 6 servings.)*

Derby Time in Louisville
The first Saturday in May.

This is a wildly glorious time of year for every Kentuckian. For days before the big day, every household readies its best linens, polishes the silver, and gets the house looking its best for the social whirl.

Guests start arriving several days before Derby Day — the ones you know you invited during the year, and a few that you had forgotten you had invited! That's when all the going to and the giving of parties take place. You drag your guests with you from brunches, to cocktail parties, to dinners, to luncheons, and to suppers, and to the Old House, which has become a must for every out-of-towner. In short, the entertaining is lavish, and everybody tries to outdo one another.

Then the big day with the big moment arrives. At five o'clock in the afternoon comes the "running for the roses," plus a sizable winner's stake, at Churchill Downs. The flags wave, the bands play, and the Derby entrants come trotting out on the track. "My Old Kentucky Home" is played, and the crowd surges to its feet in hysterical emotion. Then the horses are out of the chute and the crowd goes wild! In a few minutes it's all over, and with a gigantic sigh the mob sits down and quietly watches the pageant of the presentation of the famed blanket of roses (real ones) over the winner's neck, together with a gigantic bouquet into the arms of the victorious jockey. Of course, the lucky owners of the gallant nag are somewhat prominent, too.

What a day! Especially if you have a winning ticket! Not everyone can pick the Derby winner.

Not only the who's who of America are present, but of the whole world. Top-ranking VIP's from all over jostle each other with the traditional Kentucky mint juleps in their hands. Television cameras, movie cameras, and news cameras are busy clicking away, while the well-known press personnel are broadcasting away. All in all, the Kentucky Derby is something that everyone should experience at least once during a lifetime.

Kentucky Derby Buffet Breakfast

STIRRUP CUP
WHISKEY SOUR

OLD KENTUCKY HAM
OLD KENTUCKY HAM CROQUETTES
KETUCKY BIBB
OR
LIMESTONE LETTUCE SALAD

EGGS A LA CARDINAL HILL
BROILED DEVILED TOMATOES
HOT CHEESE BREAD

MINTED STRAWBERRY PYRAMID
BOURBON BALLS

❋ Derby Day Breakfast

In Louisville most people serve a buffet breakfast for their Derby guests about noon on Derby Saturday. The number of guests may run from six to two hundred, and the breakfast — and table decoration — tend to be about as fancy as the hostess can manage.

Stirrup Cup

In a large bowl blend together 1 cup brown sugar, 1 pint fresh lime juice, and 1 quart pineapple juice. Let mixture ripen for at least 3 hours. At serving time, pour it over a large block of ice in a punch bowl and add 4 fifths of golden or light rum. Stir thoroughly. *(Makes 25 to 30 punch cups.)*

Whiskey Sour

Juice of ½ lemon
½ teaspoon confectioners'
sugar

2 ounces bourbon whiskey
Club soda

Shake juice, sugar, and whiskey well with cracked ice and strain into 6-ounce glass. Fill with soda. Decorate with a half-slice of orange and a cherry.

Old Kentucky Ham

Let ham stand in cold water to cover overnight. Next morning, drain, cover again with cold water. To a 12- or 15-pound ham, add 2 cups brown sugar and ½ cup mixed pickling spices. Bring to a boil and simmer for about 4 or 5 hours. Take from stove and let cool in own liquor, usually overnight. Remove from liquor, cut off skin, and trim off excess fat. The ham may be decorated with cherries, pineapple slices, apricot halves, cloves, and brown sugar, and put under the broiler long enough to glaze and brown it. When ham is completely cold, cut in paper-thin slices and serve with beaten biscuits.

Old Kentucky Ham Croquettes

This is a delicious way to use up ham scraps, if there are any!

Put ham through a food grinder or chop finely. To each cup of ground ham, add 1 cup thick white sauce, 1 tablespoon Worcestershire sauce, ½ teaspoon dry mustard, 1 egg well beaten, and enough toasted bread crumbs to mold into croquettes. Roll croquettes in crumbs and fry to a golden brown in deep fat. These may be prepared ahead, frozen, and then baked for 30 minutes in a hot oven when needed.

Kentucky Bibb or Limestone Lettuce Salad

3 heads Kentucky Bibb lettuce
5-ounce jar artichoke hearts
marinated in oil

1 ripe avocado, peeled and sliced
A few torn chicory leaves

Separate the Bibb lettuce leaves. Toss all ingredients together with French dressing. *(Makes 6 servings.)*

Eggs à la Cardinal Hill

1 cup sliced onions
1 cup sliced mushrooms
2 green peppers, sliced in thin
strips
5 tablespoons butter
1 pimiento, sliced thinly
12 hard-cooked eggs, sliced

1 cup condensed celery soup,
undiluted
¼ teaspoon marjoram
¼ teaspoon ground sage
Salt and pepper

Saute onions, mushrooms, and green peppers in butter until onions are soft but not browned. Add pimiento and cook 5 minutes longer. Take from heat and mix with eggs, celery soup, and seasonings. Mix well and add salt and pepper to taste. To serve, reheat in oven for about 20 minutes and keep hot on buffet table in a chafing dish over hot water. *(Makes 6 servings.)*

Broiled Deviled Tomatoes

Dip 6 large red tomatoes into scalding water and slip off skins. Cool and cut into halves.

Cream together 3 tablespoons butter, 1 teaspoon dry mustard, 5 teaspoons Worcestershire sauce, 3 teaspoons Tabasco sauce, 1 teaspoon grated onion, and 1 teaspoon chopped parsley. Mix well and refrigerate. Arrange tomato halves on a baking sheet, put a blob of the deviled butter on top of each, and broil 5 minutes or until tomatoes are soft. Serve in the hot butter sauce with a little fresh chopped parsley sprinkled over them. *(Makes 6 servings.)*

Hot Cheese Bread

1 loaf unsliced sandwich bread
8 tablespoons butter
2 tablespoons grated onion

2 tablespoons prepared mustard
1 tablespoon sesame seed
Thin slices Swiss cheese

Remove all crust but bottom crust from bread loaf. Make diagonal cuts 1 inch apart almost through the loaf. Soften butter, blend in onion, mustard, and sesame seed. Spread on slices, saving some for the outside. Put a paper-thin slice of Swiss cheese between every 2 bread slices and press loaf together. Spread outside with butter mixture and bake uncovered at 400 degrees for 15 or 20 minutes.

Minted Strawberry Pyramid

Dip extra large, unstemmed, fresh strawberries in white corn syrup, then roll alternately in powdered sugar and chopped fresh mint. Form a pyramid on a bed of fresh mint.

Bourbon Balls

1 cup finely crushed vanilla
  wafers (about 30)
1 cup confectioners' sugar
2 tablespoons cocoa

1 cup finely chopped pecans
1½ tablespoons white corn
  syrup
2 ounces bourbon whiskey

Mix wafers well with sugar, cocoa, and nuts. Dissolve syrup in whiskey and add to dry ingredients. Blend well and form into small balls. Roll in sifted confectioners' sugar. Put in a covered container and store in the refrigerator until ready to use. *(Makes 16 walnut-sized balls.)*

Country-Style Kentucky Derby Breakfast

KENTUCKY MINT JULEP

OLD KENTUCKY HAM STEAKS
WITH RED-EYE GRAVY
EGGS AU GRATIN
HOMINY GRITS SOUFFLE
KENTUCKY CORN STICKS

COFFEE LACED WITH BOURBON

Kentucky Mint Julep

Mint   **Bourbon whiskey**
1 teaspoon sugar

Bruise or mash several sprigs of fresh mint with sugar in the bottom of a glass, preferably a silver julep cup. Add a teaspoon of water and stir until sugar is dissolved. Fill cup with crushed ice and stir well. Fill cup with good bourbon and stir. Push a small bunch of fresh mint down into ice on one side of the cup, letting mint protrude a few inches. The cup or glass will frost up, and nothing is more satisfying than sniffing the mint aroma while sipping the julep!

Old Kentucky Ham Steaks with Red-Eye Gravy

Cut steaks about a quarter of an inch thick from center of an Old Kentucky ham (one year old is best). Place an iron skillet over direct heat until it is red hot. Sear both sides of each ham steak and immediately cover with hot or cold coffee. Cover skillet, turn heat down, and simmer for 30 minutes, or until the ham steak is tender. Remove from skillet and pour skillet juices over steak.

Eggs au Gratin

4 tablespoons butter	½ teaspoon coarsely ground
1 tablespoon grated onion	black pepper
3 tablespoons minced green	¼ teaspoon nutmeg
pepper	6 hard-cooked eggs, sliced
4 tablespoons flour	2 tablespoons chopped red
3 cups scalded light cream	pimiento (canned)
3 tablespoons peeled and finely	3 tablespoons dry sherry
chopped mushrooms	Dry bread crumbs
1 teaspoon salt	Grated cheese

Melt butter, add onion and green pepper, and cook a few minutes, stirring constantly. Stir in flour and, when well blended and bubbling, stir in cream. Add mushrooms and seasonings. When sauce has thickened, place over hot water and cook 5 minutes more, stirring frequently. To sauce add eggs, pimiento, and sherry. Cook over hot water until mixture is heated thoroughly. Pour into a buttered casserole, and sprinkle with crumbs and grated cheese. Brown quickly under broiler. *(Makes 6 servings.)*

Hominy Grits Soufflé

Pour ¾ cup hominy grits into 1 cup rapidly boiling water and cook for 5 minutes, stirring constantly. Stir in 1 cup milk, place over boiling water, and cook 30 minutes. Remove from heat and stir in another cup milk and ¼ cup melted butter. Place this again over boiling water, and stir until mixture is smooth and heated through.

Remove from heat and stir in the well-beaten yolks of 4 eggs. Cool to lukewarm and fold in the stiffly beaten whites of 6 eggs. Bake in a buttered baking dish for 45 minutes in a moderate oven. *(Makes 6 servings.)*

Kentucky Corn Sticks

2 cups buttermilk	1½ cups yellow cornmeal
½ teaspoon salt	¼ cup sifted flour
½ teaspoon soda	1 egg
½ teaspoon baking powder	2 tablespoons hot shortening
1 teaspoon sugar	1 tablespoon bourbon whiskey

Put buttermilk into bowl and add salt, soda, baking powder, and sugar. Stir well. Sift cornmeal and flour together into the mixture and stir well. Add egg and beat. Add hot shortening and bourbon. Stir well. Pour into a greased corn-stick pan, filling corn-stick molds only ⅔ full to allow sticks to rise in baking. Bake at 400 degrees for 30 minutes, or until browned on top. *(Makes 14 corn sticks.)*

Coffee Laced with Bourbon

1 cup steaming black coffee	1 jigger of bourbon whiskey

Add whiskey to coffee and sugar to taste for those who like it.

TV Derby Supper

BOURBON PUNCH
MOCK KENTUCKY HAM

BLACK BEAN CASSEROLE
COTTAGE CHEESE SALAD
WITH HONEY SALAD DRESSING
KENTUCKY SALLY LUNN

BOURBON CAKE
FROSTED COFFEE
KENTUCKY BOURBON PRALINES

❋ *TV Derby Supper*

Here's a festive buffet supper for horse-race fans in other parts of the country who will get their Kentucky Derby excitement via their television sets.

Bourbon Punch

2 cups sugar	1 pint chilled lemon juice
1 pint strong iced tea	1 quart chilled ginger ale
1 pint chilled pineapple juice	1 quart good bourbon whiskey
1 quart chilled orange juice	Mint

Boil sugar with 1 pint water for 10 minutes to make a syrup, and use that to sweeten the punch to your own taste. Mix all ingredients. Float sprigs of fresh mint on top of bowl or in cups. *(Makes 20 cups.)*

Mock Kentucky Ham

Half or whole precooked
   smoked ham
1 cup dark brown sugar
1 tablespoon dry mustard
1 tablespoon Morton's Smoked
   Curing Salt

1 teaspoon coarsely ground
   black pepper
¼ teaspoon ground cloves
¼ teaspoon ground cinnamon
¼ teaspoon ground nutmeg

With an icepick, prick the ham all over, as deeply as you can. Mix remaining ingredients with just enough water to make a thick paste and spread thickly over ham. Wrap ham in foil and bake at 350 degrees for 30 minutes. Unwrap and brown quickly under broiler flame. This delicious ham may be served hot or cold.

Black Bean Casserole

2 pounds (3 cups) black beans,
   soaked overnight in water
   to cover
2 onions, sliced
1 teaspoon salt
½ teaspoon pepper

6 sprigs fresh parsley
2 bay leaves
2 stalks of celery with leaves
1 tablespoon flour
1 tablespoon butter
4 tablespoons dark rum

Leave beans in water in which they were soaked, add vegetables and seasonings, and cook till beans are soft. Add a little more water if necessary, but beans should cook down almost dry. Spoon cooked beans into a buttered casserole. Thicken the liquid left with the flour creamed to a paste with the butter. Add rum and pour over beans. Bake at 350 degrees for 30 minutes. *(Makes 6 servings.)*

Cottage Cheese Salad

2 cups creamed cottage cheese
2 tablespoons chopped chives
1 tablespoon minced onion
1 teaspoon Worcestershire sauce

2 tablespoons chopped parsley
2 tablespoons chopped green
   pepper
½ cup finely chopped nuts

Mix all ingredients except nuts and pile on lettuce. Sprinkle with chopped nuts and serve with Honey Salad Dressing on top. *(Makes 6 servings.)*

Honey Salad Dressing

1 egg	1 clove garlic, minced
1 tablespoon warm honey	½ teaspoon salt
¼ teaspoon ground ginger	¼ teaspoon coarsely ground
1 teaspoon dry mustard	black pepper
2 tablespoons lemon juice	1 cup salad oil

Put all ingredients into blender or mixer bowl except ¾ cup oil. Mix on slow speed for half a minute, then slowly add ¾ cup oil steadily. (Can also be made with hand beater.) *(Makes about 1½ cups.)*

Kentucky Sally Lunn

2 eggs, separated	¼ cup sugar
½ cup milk	½ teaspoon salt
½ cake yeast	2 cups flour
½ cup butter	

Beat egg yolks and whites separately and well. Heat milk to lukewarm and mix with yeast. Cream butter and sugar. Add yolks, salt, and flour, alternating with milk-yeast mixture. Fold in egg whites. Put in a greased pie pan and let stand until double in bulk (2 to 3 hours). Bake 30 minutes at 375 degrees. When bread is done, remove from oven, cut into pie-shaped wedges, and spread with butter while hot.

Bourbon Cake

1½ cups flour	3 eggs, separated
1 teaspoon baking powder	2 teaspoons nutmeg
½ pound chopped seedless	½ cup bourbon whiskey
raisins	1 pound chopped pecans
8 tablespoons butter	Salt
1 cup sugar	

Sift flour and baking powder and mix with raisins. Cream butter and sugar until light and fluffy. Add egg yolks one at a time, beating well until the mixture is smooth and lemon-colored. Soak nutmeg in bourbon. Add spiced liquor gradually along with flour and raisins to creamed mixture. Beat thoroughly to blend batter. Fold in nuts. Beat egg whites stiffly with a pinch of salt and fold into batter. Butter a tube pan large enough to hold a 3-pound cake. Line it with buttered paper. Pour the batter into the pan and let it stand to settle a few minutes. Bake at 350 degrees for 1½ hours. If top browns too quickly, cover it with a piece of foil. Let cake stand in pan ½ hour before removing it to a cake rack to cool completely. When cool, cover cake with Bourbon Icing.

Bourbon Icing

Grated rind and juice of 2
    lemons
4 cups confectioners' sugar
8 tablespoons butter or
    margarine, softened

1 teaspoon cream
2 tablespoons bourbon whiskey

Add lemon juice and rind to sugar, mix, and let stand about 10 minutes. Blend butter and sugar together. Beat in cream and whiskey.

Frosted Coffee

6 tablespoons instant coffee
½ cup sugar
6 cups boiling water
1-inch stick of cinnamon
8 whole cloves

2 whole allspice
½ cup heavy cream
3 tablespoons confectioners'
    sugar
1 teaspoon vanilla

Combine coffee and sugar in a pitcher. Pour boiling water over. Stir to dissolve sugar. Add spices. Let stand for 1 hour. Strain out spices. Chill. Whip cream until stiff. Stir in confectioners' sugar and vanilla. Pour spiced coffee into tall glasses over ice cubes. Top with whipped cream.

Kentucky Bourbon Pralines

2 cups sugar
1 teaspoon baking soda
1 cup buttermilk
Pinch of salt

2 tablespoons butter or
    margarine
2½ cups pecan halves
2½ ounces bourbon whiskey

In a large kettle combine the first 4 ingredients. Cook 5 minutes over light heat, stirring constantly. Add butter and pecans. Cook, stirring constantly and scraping bottom and sides of kettle, until mixture forms a soft ball in cold water. Remove from heat and add bourbon. Allow to cool a few minutes, then beat by hand about 5 minutes. When mixture begins to thicken slightly, drop by tablespoonfuls onto waxed paper. Let cool and harden.

A Kentucky Burgoo

BURGOO
SKILLET CORN BREAD

GINGERBREAD
WITH BOURBON SAUCE

AFTER-DINNER APPLE TODDY

❋ Kentucky Burgoo

Back in pioneer days, burgoo was a very important item in Kentucky lives. All the well-to-do settlers toted their huge iron pots with them, either across the mountains or, in later years, by barge down the Ohio River from Pittsburgh. Some of these iron pots were gigantic, holding as much as fifty gallons and serving many purposes. Usually a long green log was wedged in the crotch of two trees twelve to fifteen feet apart and the pot was suspended by chains from this log. The log was wedged high enough so that a good-sized fire could be kept beneath the kettle. In the late fall, hogs, either wild or otherwise, were scalded in it. At other times lye soap was made in it from wood ashes. Every Monday, without fail, the family wash was boiled in it. Between these various necessities, the burgoo bubbled in it.

The Kentucky hunters with their long squirrel rifles were the main providers of the burgoo. Squirrels, grouse, wild turkeys, deer, and quail were bagged, dressed, and thrown into the iron pot. In cold weather, wild porkers and rabbits added their flavors. Along with these went turnips, carrots, onions, corn, dried beans, and any wild greens such as young polk shoots, burdock, and lamb's quarter. This simmered hour upon hour, for days, and produced a thick souplike stew with the meats shredded all through it.

Here is a modern version of that flavory stew.

Burgoo

2 pounds lean beef with bone	2 cups diced onions
1 medium-size stewing chicken	1 pint butter beans
1 pound veal	3 large carrots, diced
4 quarts water	1 clove garlic, mashed
2 cups chopped okra	1 cup minced fresh parsley
2 green peppers, chopped	1 bunch celery, chopped with
1 small red pepper	leaves
1 quart tomatoes	Salt and pepper to taste
6 ears corn cut off cob	3 cups dry sherry
2 cups diced raw potatoes	

Boil beef, chicken, and veal in water until very tender. Remove meat from bones and replace meat in pot. Add other ingredients except sherry and cook over slow heat for 2 hours. The mixture should be very thick. Stir it up from the bottom occasionally. Before serving, add sherry and stir well. *(Makes 12 servings.)*

Skillet Corn Bread

In an iron skillet fry 1 pound ground pork-sausage meat, stirring until meat is done. Pour off grease.

Scald 2 cups coarse yellow cornmeal with 1 cup boiling water. Add 1 teaspoon salt and the cooked sausage. Put ¼ teaspoon baking soda in ¾ cup buttermilk and add to cornmeal mixture. Return to skillet.

Bake in preheated oven at 400 degrees, 15 to 20 minutes, or until a broom straw inserted in the middle comes out clean and corn bread is brown on top. Cut and serve in wedges. *(Makes 6 servings.)*

Gingerbread

½ cup bacon drippings	½ teaspoon salt
1 cup brown sugar	1½ teaspoons ginger
2 eggs	½ cup boiling water
1 teaspoon grated lemon rind	½ cup molasses (sorghum is
2 cups sifted flour	best, or dark brown)
1 teaspoon nutmeg	2 tablespoons bourbon whiskey
1 teaspoon baking soda	

Cream bacon grease and sugar together. Beat eggs in one at a time. Add grated lemon rind. Sift flour with nutmeg, baking soda, salt, and ginger. Combine boiling water and molasses in a bowl. Add sifted and liquid ingredients alternately to creamed mixture. Beat after each addition; blend in whiskey last. Pour into a greased, lightly floured pan and bake 40 minutes at 350 degrees. Serve hot with Bourbon Sauce. *(Makes 6 servings.)*

Bourbon Sauce

2 cups brown sugar
1 tablespoon butter
1 heaping tablespoon flour

1 cup hot water
½ cup bourbon whiskey

Cream sugar, butter, and flour together, Add water a little at a time. Put in a double boiler and cook until thick. When sauce cools to warm, add whiskey. Spread over gingerbread.

After-Dinner Apple Toddy

Quarter and peel 1 apple. Put in a saucepan, cover with water, and stew until apple is tender. Add ½ cup sugar to make syrup. Add 1 tablespoon butter, a good shake of nutmeg, and boil rapidly for a few minutes.

To serve: Put a tablespoon of the apple mixture in an Old-Fashioned glass and add 1 jigger of bourbon whiskey. Serve hot.

Mother's Day Dinner

LUXURY COCKTAIL
SHERRY COBBLER
SHERRY MILK PUNCH

PA'S CHICKEN SCALLOP FOR MA
SISTER'S FLOWERS FOR MOTHER (SALAD)
BROTHER'S VEGETABLE HULLABALOO

APPLESAUCE CRUNCH

✸ Mother's Day

On "her day" Mother should be the queen bee and let the other members of the hive do the work. The following recipes can be easily put together by the master of the house and by the teen-agers.

Luxury Cocktail

3 ounces brandy   3 ounces well-chilled champagne
2 dashes orange bitters

Stir lightly.

Sherry Cobbler

1 teaspoon confectioners' sugar   3 ounces dry sherry
2 ounces club soda

Put sugar and soda in 10-ounce glass or goblet with shaved ice. Add sherry. Stir well and decorate with fruits in season. Serve with straws.

Sherry Milk Punch

1 teaspoon confectioners' sugar   ½ pint milk
3 ounces dry sherry

Shake with cracked ice, strain into tall glass, and grate nutmeg on top.

Pa's Chicken Scallop for Ma

2 tablespoons chopped onion   ¼ teaspoon poultry seasoning
2 cups chopped celery   ½ teaspoon salt
Butter or margarine   ¼ teaspoon pepper
¼ cup flour   2 cups chopped cooked chicken
2 cups milk   1 cup finely chopped cooked
1 cup broth from 1 whole   ham
    canned chicken   3 cups cheese-flavored cracker
3 tablespoons finely chopped   crumbs
    parsley

Heat oven to 425 degrees. Saute onion and celery in butter until tender. Stir in flour. Add milk and broth gradually, stirring until smooth and thickened. Add parsley, seasonings, chicken, and ham. Place a thick layer of crumbs in the bottom of a 2½-quart greased casserole, then a layer of creamed mixture, and repeat. Sprinkle remaining crumbs on top. Dot with butter and bake uncovered for 20 minutes, or until crumbs are browned. *(Serves 6.)*

Sister's Flowers for Mother (Salad)

1 package of lime gelatin   ½ teaspoon salt
¼ cup hot water plus ¾ cup   1 teaspoon lemon juice
    cold water   1 cup heavy cream, whipped
1 cucumber, pared and diced   18 radishes

Dissolve gelatin in hot water; add cold water. Combine cucumber, salt, and lemon juice. Cool. Mix lime gelatin and whipped cream. Pour into 6 small custard molds or cups and chill thoroughly until firm. Unmold with flat sides up to look like flower pots.

Prepare radish roses: Slice the peeling on four sides of each radish halfway down and press open. Place 3 radish roses on top of each green flower pot and put a blob of mayonnaise on the side. *(Makes 6 servings.)*

70

Brother's Vegetable Hullabaloo

4 potatoes, peeled and thinly
    sliced
1 small eggplant, cubed
4 tomatoes, coarsely chopped
2 onions, coarsely chopped
3 green peppers, coarsely
    chopped
3 carrots, coarsely chopped

3 cloves garlic, chopped
4 sprigs fresh parsley, chopped
1 teaspoon basil
1 level teaspoon salt
¼ teaspoon pepper
2 cups water
Butter

Butter a baking dish and arrange potato slices and eggplant cubes in layers on the bottom. Combine chopped vegetables and seasonings, and spread over potatoes and eggplant. Pour water over vegetables and bake at 375 degrees about 45 minutes, or until potatoes are tender. Dot top of vegetables with bits of butter and bake a few minutes longer. *(Makes 6 servings.)*

Applesauce Crunch

2 cans (1 pound each) or 3 cups
    sweetened applesauce
½ teaspoon almond extract
2 tablespoons grated lemon peel
3 tablespoons softened butter or
    margarine
⅓ cup dark brown sugar,
    firmly packed

⅓ cup fine graham-cracker
    crumbs
⅓ cup slivered, blanched
    almonds
Dash of salt

Heat oven to 400 degrees. Combine applesauce, almond extract, and lemon peel in a greased, shallow, 1-quart baking dish. Blend butter, brown sugar, graham-crackers crumbs, slivered almonds, and salt. Sprinkle mixture evenly over applesauce and bake for 10 minutes. Turn oven on broil, and broil top until it is brown and crusty. Serve warm or cold. *(Serves 4 to 6.)*

Father's Day Dinner

SIR WALTER COCKTAIL
OLD PAL COCKTAIL

BEER CHEDDAR SOUP

POP'S FAVORITE HAMBURGERS
CABBAGE IN BEER
FRIED POTATOES

LETTUCE AND LEEK SALAD

BANANA TRIFLE

Sir Walter Cocktail

¾ ounce imported rum
¾ ounce brandy
1 teaspoon grenadine

1 teaspoon curaçao
1 teaspoon lemon juice

Shake well with cracked ice and strain into cocktail glass.

Old Pal Cocktail

1¼ ounces rye or bourbon
  whiskey

½ ounce applejack
½ ounce pure maple syrup

Shake with cracked ice and strain into cocktail glass.

Beer Cheddar Soup

1 quart beer
2 tablespoons butter
2 tablespoons flour
½ teaspoon salt
¼ teaspoon coarsely ground
  black pepper

1 clove garlic
2 egg yolks
3 tablespoons sour cream
1¼ cups grated cheddar cheese

Bring beer to a boil. Cream butter, flour, salt, pepper, and garlic and gradually stir into beer. Beat egg yolks lightly with sour cream and add to soup. Add 1 cup cheese and simmer until cheese is melted. Pour over toast in soup bowls and sprinkle with remaining cheddar. If a thinner soup is desired, stir in a little more beer just before serving and correct seasoning to taste. *(Makes 6 servings.)*

Pop's Favorite Hamburgers

3 medium-sized boiled potatoes
1 pound ground chuck
1 egg, beaten
1 ounce (¼ cup) pine nuts
½ cup dried currants

½ teaspoon chopped thyme
½ teaspoon chopped dill
½ teaspoon chopped parsley
Tomato sauce
Salt and pepper to taste

Mash potatoes with a fork; add ground meat. Stir in beaten egg. Add nuts, currants, herbs, salt, and pepper. Mix together and form into round flat cakes about 2 inches across. Fry in deep fat until brown. Serve with tomato sauce. *(Makes 6 servings.)*

Cabbage in Beer

1 small head cabbage
2 large green peppers
1 large Bermuda onion

2 tablespoons bacon drippings
1 bottle warm beer
Salt and pepper to taste

Cut up cabbage coarsely, slice peppers and onion. Saute cabbage, peppers, and onion in drippings a few minutes, turning to coat all with fat. Add salt and pepper. Pour beer over all, cover, and simmer over low heat until beer has been absorbed by vegetables and cabbage and onions are tender. *(Makes 6 servings.)*

Fried Potatoes

1½ pounds or 4 to 6 medium-sized potatoes	1 tablespoon olive oil
	¼ teaspoon ground nutmeg
1 tablespoon butter	Salt and pepper to taste

Peel and slice potatoes very thin. Wash in cold water and dry. Melt butter and oil in a large skillet. When hot, arrange potatoes flatly. Add nutmeg, salt, and pepper. Fry for about 5 minutes, turning several times. Lower heat, cover pan, and cook for 15 minutes. Turn potatoes over and continue cooking until tender and browned on each side. Serve whole as a pancake or cut into wedges. *(Makes 6 servings.)*

Lettuce and Leek Salad

1 small head lettuce	2 tablespoons wine vinegar
2 large leeks	1 teaspoon sugar
4 strips bacon	Salt and pepper

Shred lettuce and chop leeks, stems and all. Dice bacon in small pieces and fry until crisp. Stir vinegar into bacon fat and add sugar, salt, and pepper. Pour over lettuce and leeks. Serve at once, while still hot. *(Makes 6 servings.)*

Banana Trifle

7 bananas	3 tablespoons dry sherry
2 tablespoons apricot jam	½ pint whipped cream

Peel and cut 6 bananas lengthwise. Spread with jam and pour over sherry. Let stand for 1 hour. To serve, top with whipped cream and decorate with 1 banana sliced into very thin rounds. *(Makes 6 servings.)*

Bridal Shower Luncheon

SPICED TEA PUNCH

FRENCH SALT STICKS
SOUTH SEA CHICKEN
SAVORY TOMATO MOLDS

FROZEN RAINBOW TORTES
WITH RUBY SAUCE

Spiced Tea Punch

1 quart water	1½ cups sugar
2 heaping tablespoons loose tea or 7 tea bags	1 cup orange juice
½ teaspoon nutmeg	½ cup lemon juice
½ teaspoon ground cinnamon	1 quart cold cranberry juice cocktail
½ teaspoon allspice	1 quart chilled club soda

Bring water to a boil. Remove from heat. Immediately add tea, nutmeg, cinnamon, and allspice. Cover and steep 10 minutes. Stir and strain into a punch bowl containing sugar and fruit juices. Just before serving add ice cubes and soda. *(Makes 35 punch cups.)*

French Salt Sticks

2 tablespoons sugar
1 tablespoon salt
1 quart water
2 ounces (½ stick) butter or
   margarine

3 ounces yeast
12 cups hard-wheat flour

Add sugar and salt to water; mix. Add shortening. Add yeast and flour; mix to a stiff dough. Roll dough to size and length desired. Cut dough into strips and roll between your palms. Bake until lightly browned at 425 degrees. While hot, sprinkle with salt. *(Makes 24 to 30 salt sticks.)*

South Sea Chicken

24 boned chicken breasts
12 fresh ripe pineapples
1 pound butter
2 cups flour
6 cups chicken stock
6 cups cream
3 cups dry sherry

3 cups Cointreau (or other
   orange-flavored liqueur)
4 cups sliced cooked or canned
   mushrooms, drained
Rock salt
4 cups toasted sliced almonds
4 cups toasted coconut

Cook chicken breasts in small amount of water to obtain a well-seasoned, strong stock. Remove breasts and cut into 1-inch cubes. Split pineapples in half lengthwise, leaving stem leaves on. Hollow out, leaving half of fruit in shell. Score fruit in shell and loosen, leaving in place in shell. Mince pineapple removed from shell and set aside.

Make a roux of butter and flour (creamed together). Add stock, minced pineapple, and cream. Simmer gently for a few minutes until pineapple becomes soft. Do not boil, or cream will curdle. Add sherry, Cointreau, mushrooms, and diced chicken. Simmer until well blended. Season to taste.

Turn mixture into pineapple halves on top of loosened fruit. Set pineapple shells on beds of rock salt. Bake at 350 degrees until pineapple shells are thoroughly heated. Sprinkle generously with toasted almonds and coconut. Serve in pineapple shells on the rock salt. *(Makes 24 servings.)*

Savory Tomato Molds

24 large tomatoes, all the same size

FILLING:

3 envelopes unflavored gelatin
3 tablespoons sugar
1½ teaspoons salt
1½ cups water
3 pounds (6 cups) cottage cheese

6 tablespoons horseradish
1½ cups heavy cream, whipped
6 cups diced unpeeled red apples
¾ cup diced green pepper

Dip tomatoes into boiling water and slip skins from them. Scoop seeds and pulp from tomatoes and place them on tray in refrigerator to chill.

Mix gelatin, sugar, and salt thoroughly in a saucepan. Add water. Place over low heat and stir until gelatin is dissolved. Sieve or beat cottage cheese on high speed of electric mixer. Blend in gelatin mixture. Fold in remaining ingredients.

Take tomato cups from refrigerator and sprinkle insides with salt and pepper. Fill tomato cups with cottage cheese mixture, piling lightly on top. Sprinkle tops with coarsely ground black pepper and return to refrigerator to chill until filling is firm. Serve on greens such as parsley, curly endive, or watercress. *(Makes 24 servings.)*

Frozen Rainbow Tortes

2¼ cups egg whites (from 6 to 8 eggs)
2 tablespoons vanilla
1½ teaspoons cream of tartar
¾ teaspoon salt

3¼ cups sugar
1 gallon strawberry ice cream
½ gallon pistachio ice cream
1½ quarts heavy or double-thick cream

Beat egg whites, vanilla, cream of tartar, and salt until foamy. Add sugar gradually, beating until very stiff. Pipe or spread meringue onto paper-covered baking sheets to form twelve 8-inch circles. Bake in a 275-degree oven 1 hour. Turn off heat and let stand in oven at least 1 hour. Cool. Lift meringues from paper. Chill.

Let ice cream stand at room temperature until slightly softened. Spread about 1¼ pints strawberry ice cream on each of 6 meringue layers. Place in freezer. Spread pistachio ice cream over 3 layers of meringue. Stack ice-cream-covered layers to form 3 tortes with pistachio layer in middle. Top each torte with one of remaining layers of meringue.

Hold in freezer while whipping topping. Whip cream until peaks form. Frost tortes and freeze at least 4 hours, preferably overnight. Just before serving, drizzle tortes with Ruby Sauce and serve with additional sauce. *(Makes three 8-inch tortes.)*

Ruby Sauce

6½ pounds frozen whole
   strawberries
Cornstarch, 1 tablespoon for
  each cup strawberry juice

¼ cup grated orange rind
Orange extract to taste

Thaw berries; drain. Measure juice. Thicken juice with cornstarch. Cool mixture. Add to berries. Blend in orange rind. Stir in orange extract, tasting for flavor.

Bridesmaids' Luncheon

PINK LADY
CLARET LEMONADE

SPAGHETTI BOTTICELLI
AVOCADO SALAD
WITH PARMESAN CHEESE DRESSING

SWEET POTATO SHORTCAKE WEDDING BELLS
PEPPERMINT WHIP

Pink Lady

1½ ounces gin   1 egg white or 3 ounces cream
2 teaspoons grenadine

Shake well with ice and strain into cocktail glass.

Claret Lemonade

Juice of 1 lemon   2 ounces claret
2 teaspoons confectioners' sugar

Put lemon juice and sugar in 12-ounce glass and fill with shaved ice. Add enough water to fill glass, leaving room to float wine on top. Decorate with slices of orange and lemon, and a cherry. Serve with straws.

Spaghetti Botticelli

2 tablespoons olive oil	¼ teaspoon dried basil
½ pound pork sausage	½ bay leaf
1 pound lean ground beef	¼ teaspoon dried thyme
1 cup chopped onion	½ teaspoon pepper
1 clove garlic, minced	1 tablespoon salt
3½ cups Italian-style tomatoes	1 cup chopped ripe olives
6-ounce can tomato paste	½ pound spaghetti
1 cup rich beef stock or bouillon	¼ cup capers
2 tablespoons chopped parsley	

Heat oil in a saucepan and brown sausage and beef. Add onion, garlic, and tomatoes and cook for 10 minutes. Add tomato paste, stock, parsley, and seasonings and simmer 1 hour. Add olives cut in large pieces; add capers. Cook spaghetti in boiling salted water according to package directions until tender. Drain. Spoon meat sauce over and mix lightly with a fork. Turn into a shallow 2½-quart greased casserole and bake uncovered at 350 degrees for 30 minutes. *(Makes 6 servings.)*

Avocado Salad

Chill 3 fully ripe and soft avocados. Cut in half and discard stones. Peel halves and cut into thin slices. Toss lightly with 1 tablespoon lemon juice and refrigerate in a covered dish. Drain one 5- or 6-ounce can of water chestnuts, slice thinly, and add to sliced avocados. Tear up ½-head iceberg lettuce and 1 bunch watercress, and add 1 cup torn small young spinach leaves. Add to avocados and water chestnuts, toss lightly, and refrigerate in a covered bowl until ready to serve. Serve with Parmesan Cheese Dressing. *(Serves 6.)*

Parmesan Cheese Dressing

½ cup tarragon vinegar	1 teaspoon chopped parsley
¾ teaspoon salt	1 teaspoon chervil
¼ teaspoon coarsely ground black pepper	½ teaspoon dry mustard
1½ cups olive oil	4 tablespoons grated Parmesan cheese

Mix vinegar, salt, pepper, and oil; beat until thick. Add parsley, chervil, and mustard, and mix well. Stir in cheese. Do not refrigerate — keep at room temperature until ready to use. *(Makes 2½ cups.)*

Sweet Potato Shortcake Wedding Bells

1 cup sifted flour
1 teaspoon baking powder
½ teaspoon salt
⅓ cup melted butter

1 cup cold mashed canned sweet
  potato
1 egg, well beaten

Sift flour with baking powder and salt. Work in mashed sweet potato, butter, and egg. Roll ¼-inch thick. With a cookie cutter, cut dough into small bells. Bake at 450 degrees on a greased baking sheet for 15 to 20 minutes, or until browned. *(Makes 6 servings.)*

Peppermint Whip

14 chocolate wafers, finely
  crushed
1¼ cups miniature
  marshmallows

½ cup crushed hard
  peppermint candy
½ pint heavy cream, whipped

Cover bottom of 9x9-inch dish with half the chocolate crumbs. Fold marshmallows and candy into whipped cream and carefully spoon onto crumbs. Sprinkle remaining crumbs on top and refrigerate for at least 12 hours. *(Makes 6 servings.)*

Friday Bridesmaids' Luncheon

DUBONNET PUNCH
CUPID COCKTAIL

CRAB NEWBURG
CHERRY MOLDED SALAD
WAX BEANS WITH DILL

STRAWBERRY SWIRL

Dubonnet Punch

Juice of 1 dozen lemons	1 pint brandy
Confectioners' sugar	1 pint rum
1 quart club soda	1 pint champagne
2 quarts Dubonnet wine	½ pint sweet vermouth

Sweeten lemon juice with sugar. Place in punch bowl with large block of ice and stir well, then add rest of ingredients. Stir well and decorate with fruits in season. Serve in punch cups. *(Makes about 30 punch cups.)*

Cupid Cocktail

2 ounces dry sherry	1 teaspoon confectioners' sugar
1 egg	

Shake well with cracked ice and strain into champagne glass. Grate a little nutmeg on top.

Crab Newburg

4 tablespoons butter
½ cup chopped onion
1 clove garlic, finely minced
2 tablespoons flour
2 cups crabmeat
1½ cups cream
1 tablespoon chopped green onion tops

1 green pepper, chopped
1 teaspoon chopped parsley
⅛ teaspoon thyme
⅛ teaspoon freshly ground black pepper
Salt to taste
¼ cup dry sherry

Put butter into saucepan and melt. Saute onion and garlic until soft but not browned. Stir in flour. Add crabmeat and cream. Add green pepper, onion tops, parsley, thyme, pepper, and salt to taste. Cook for 15 minutes over low heat, stirring constantly. Just before serving, stir in sherry. Serve over split toasted muffins. *(Makes 6 servings.)*

Cherry Molded Salad

2 packages (3 ounces each) cherry-flavored gelatin
1½ cups hot water
1½ cups Coca-Cola or other cola drink

3½ cups black pitted cherries and their juice
3½ cups crushed pineapple, drained

Dissolve gelatin in hot water, add Coca-Cola, black cherries, and juice. Add pineapple. Refrigerate until firm. Serve with mayonnaise on salad greens. *(Makes 6 servings.)*

Wax Beans with Dill

6 tablespoons chopped pimiento
6 tablespoons chopped onion
4 tablespoons bacon drippings
¼ teaspoon salt

⅛ teaspoon black pepper
4 cups cooked wax beans
¼ cup water
2 tablespoons chopped dill

Cook pimiento and onion in fat 3 minutes. Add salt, pepper, and beans. Add water. Simmer over low heat 15 minutes. Take from heat, drain, and stir in dill. *(Makes 6 servings.)*

Strawberry Swirl

1 cup crisp chocolate cookie crumbs

4 tablespoons butter

9-inch pie shell

1 tablespoon sugar

2 cups sliced fresh strawberries

3-ounce package strawberry gelatin

1 cup boiling water

½ pound marshmallows

½ cup milk

1 cup whipping cream

Combine crumbs and butter and press into a 9-inch pie shell. Sprinkle sugar over berries. Let stand 30 minutes. Dissolve gelatin in boiling water. Drain berries, reserving juice. Add water to juice to make 1 cup and add to gelatin. Chill until partially set. Heat marshmallows and milk, stirring until marshmallows melt. Cool thoroughly, whip cream, and fold in. Add berries to gelatin, then swirl in marshmallow mixture. Pour into pie shell. Chill until filling is set.

Bachelor Dinner

BULL'S-EYE
BULL'S MILK
DAMN-THE-WEATHER COCKTAIL

BETWEEN THE SHEETS
ROAST BEEF IN BEER
HERBED MASHED POTATOES
WILTED LETTUCE BOWL
CHEESE BISCUITS

RUM ICEBOX PIE

"GET ME TO THE CHURCH ON TIME"
AFTER-DINNER DRINK

Bull's-Eye

1 ounce brandy	Ginger ale
2 ounces hard cider	

Put brandy and cider in 8-ounce highball glass. Add ice, fill glass with ginger ale, and stir.

Bull's Milk

1 teaspoon confectioners' sugar	1½ ounces brandy
1 ounce dark rum	½ pint milk

Shake well with cracked ice and strain into highball glass. Add a little grated nutmeg and a pinch of cinnamon on top.

Damn-the-Weather Cocktail

1 ounce curaçao
½ ounce orange juice

½ ounce sweet vermouth
1 ounce dry gin

Shake with cracked ice and strain into cocktail glass.

Between the Sheets

Juice of ¼ lemon
½ ounce Triple Sec or other
   orange-flavored liqueur

½ ounce brandy
½ ounce imported rum

Shake with cracked ice and strain into cocktail glass.

Roast Beef in Beer

Put a 5-pound pot roast of beef in a bowl. Sprinkle it with 2 tablespoons sugar, 1 tablespoon salt, ½ teaspoon powdered cloves, and 2 tablespoons freshly ground pepper. Add 1 chopped onion and 1 chopped carrot. Pour 2 bottles beer and ½ cup olive oil over meat. Place in refrigerator and let marinate overnight, turning it several times in the marinade.

For rare beef, which most men like, roast 15 to 20 minutes per pound at 400 degrees. Baste with marinade while roasting. *(Makes 6 servings.)*

Herbed Mashed Potatoes

2 cups hot mashed potatoes
   (mashed with a little milk
   or cream)
2 tablespoons butter
½ teaspoon salt

⅛ teaspoon freshly ground
   black pepper
1 teaspoon chopped parsley
½ teaspoon chervil
½ teaspoon marjoram

Mix hot potatoes, butter, and seasonings. With a pastry tube or a large spoon, make potato cones on a greased baking sheet. Brown lightly under broiler before serving. *(Makes 6 servings.)*

Wilted Lettuce Bowl

1 large head lettuce
1 cup torn fresh spinach leaves
4 slices of bacon, diced
½ cup chopped green onions
   with tops
⅛ teaspoon freshly ground
   black pepper

½ teaspoon salt
¼ cup vinegar
1 teaspoon sugar (optional)
Few fresh dandelion greens
   (optional)
Chopped hard-boiled egg

Shred lettuce and tear spinach leaves into a salad bowl. Fry bacon crisp and drain. Crumble crisp bacon onto greens. To hot bacon fat in skillet, add salt, pepper, and vinegar. If you do not like a really sour taste, stir in a little sugar. Bring to boil and pour over greens. Toss well. For a dash, add a few fresh tender dandelion leaves. Garnish top of salad with hard-boiled egg. *(Makes 6 servings.)*

Cheese Biscuits

2 cups sifted flour
¾ cup grated sharp cheddar
   or other sharp cheese
½ teaspoon salt
1 teaspoon sugar

4 teaspoons baking powder
3 tablespoons shortening
Milk to make a soft dough
   (about ¾ cup)

Mix flour, cheese, salt, sugar, and baking powder together. Cut in shortening until mixture resembles coarse crumbs. Add liquid all at once and mix just until dough follows fork around bowl. Turn out on a lightly floured surface. Pat with hand to desired thickness. Cut biscuits and bake in a hot oven (450 degrees) 15 minutes, or until browned. *(Makes 20 small biscuits.)*

Rum Icebox Pie

15 chocolate cream-filled
   cookies, crushed
⅓ cup melted butter
5 egg yolks
1 cup sugar

1 envelope unflavored gelatin
1 pint whipping cream
Dark rum
Chopped pecans

Mix cookie crumbs with melted butter and pat into a 9 x 9 pie pan; chill in refrigerator. Beat egg yolks until light and add sugar. Soak gelatin and water over low heat and bring to a boil. Pour over eggs and sugar, stirring.

Whip cream until stiff and fold into egg mixture. Add ½ cup dark rum, and mix well. Cool filling until it begins to set, then pour it into pie shell. Chill until firm. Sprinkle top with chopped pecans that have been soaked 24 hours in enough dark rum to cover them.

"Get Me to the Church on Time" After-Dinner Drink

1 ounce apricot brandy
1 ounce brandy

1 ounce curaçao
½ teaspoon lemon juice

Shake with cracked ice and strain into cocktail glass.

Small Wedding Reception

CHAMPAGNE PUNCH
WEDDING CAKE

FRUITED CHICKEN SALAD
ROQUEFORT OR BLEU CHEESE MOUSSE
STUFFED FRENCH LOAF

Champagne Punch

Juice of 1 dozen lemons
Confectioners' sugar
1 quart club soda
½ pint maraschino

½ pint curaçao
1 pint brandy
2 quarts champagne

Sweeten lemon juice with confectioners' sugar. Place large block of ice in punch bowl, add lemon juice and soda, and stir well. Add rest of ingredients and stir well. Decorate with thinly sliced strawberries floating on top. *(Makes 30 punch cups.)*

Wedding Cake

3 cups cake flour, sifted
3 teaspoons baking powder
¼ teaspoon salt
⅔ cup butter (1 stick plus
   3 teaspoons)

1½ cups sugar
1 teaspoon vanilla extract
3 egg yolks, well beaten
1 cup milk
3 egg whites, stiffly beaten

Sift together flour, baking powder, and salt. Cream butter until soft and smooth, and gradually add sugar, beating constantly until mixture is very fluffy. Beat in vanilla and egg yolks. Gradually add dry ingredients alternately with milk, beating well after each addition.

Carefully fold in egg whites. Turn batter into 4 buttered round layer-cake pans, graduated in size from 3 to 9 inches in diameter. Bake in moderate oven 20 to 30 minutes, or until a broom straw inserted into cake comes out clean. Cool cakes and put together with the following icing.

ICING:

1 pound confectioners' sugar	Juice of 1 lemon
2 egg whites	Crystallized flowers

Sift sugar through a fine sieve. In a separate bowl, combine egg whites with lemon juice. Add a little of this to sugar, working and beating well with a wooden spoon. Continue to add a little at a time until icing is mixed and smooth and creamy.

Spread a very thin layer over cakes, dipping knife in cold water. As each layer dries, put cake together with a thick layer of icing between layers, covering outside of cake as well. Use a pastry bag to decorate the edges. Decorate cake with crystallized flowers. A wedding cake may be simple or as ornate as you wish.

Fruited Chicken Salad

1 orange	1 apple, diced
15 large white seeded or seedless grapes	3 cups diced cooked white meat of chicken or turkey
15 salted almonds	1 teaspoon marjoram
1 banana	1 teaspoon thyme
1 cup mayonnaise	

Peel, seed, and remove membrane from sections of orange. Cut orange segments in half. Cut grapes in half. Split almonds, slice banana thin, and mix all ingredients lightly but thoroughly. Add mayonnaise, diced apple, and diced chicken. Add marjoram and thyme and mix well. Chill and serve very cold. *(Makes 8 servings.)*

Roquefort or Bleu Cheese Mousse

6 egg yolks	¾ pound Roquefort or bleu cheese
6 tablespoons cream	1½ cups heavy cream, whipped
1½ tablespoons gelatin	3 egg whites, stiffly beaten
4 tablespoons cold water	

Beat egg yolks with cream in saucepan over low heat until mixture is creamy. Soften gelatin in cold water. Dissolve gelatin over hot water and add to eggs. Chop cheese finely and add to gelatin mixture. Cool; fold in whipped cream and egg whites. Pour mousse into an oiled mold and chill for several hours. Unmold mousse on a platter and garnish top with watercress or mint. *(Makes 8 servings.)*

Stuffed French Loaf

Trim ends from a loaf of French (or Italian) bread and scoop out bread inside to make a long hollow tube in a ¼-inch crust. Fill loaf with the following:

Mash 6 anchovies with 3 tablespoons sweet butter and blend them with 1 cup each of diced cooked ham, Edam cheese, and ½ cup diced cooked tongue. Mix in lightly 3 small pickles, sliced, and 2 tablespoons caviar.

Wrap filled loaf in foil and chill for several hours. Cut in ¼-inch slices.

Wedding Breakfast

KISS COCKTAIL
ROYAL PURPLE PUNCH
BROILED GRAPEFRUIT WITH PORT

HERBED SHRIMP SCRAMBLE
STUFFED MUSHROOMS
BROILED TOMATOES

ORANGE BLOSSOM BISCUITS
MACAROON MOUSSE

Kiss Cocktail

¼ ounce orange juice   ¾ ounce dry vermouth
¼ ounce Dubonnet   ¾ ounce bourbon whiskey

Shake well with cracked ice and strain into cocktail glass.

Royal Purple Punch

Pour 2 fifths of claret wine and 2 quarts ginger ale over ice cubes in a punch bowl. Stir well. Float paper-thin slices of lemon studded with cloves on top.

Broiled Grapefruit with Port

Cut grapefruit in half. Seed and core. Fill core with port wine and sprinkle brown sugar over top. Broil until grapefruit is hot and the sugar has melted and crystallized a little.

Herbed Shrimp Scramble

6 eggs
1 cup cooked, peeled, and
    cleaned shrimps
1 tablespoon chopped parsley
1 teaspoon chervil
¼ teaspoon black pepper
1 teaspoon salt

4 tablespoons crisp crumbled
    bacon
1 cup cooked or canned
    asparagus, cut into small
    pieces
½ cup cream

Mix all ingredients together in mixing bowl and pour into well-buttered skillet over medium heat. Stir while cooking until eggs are of desired consistency. *(Makes 6 servings.)*

Stuffed Mushrooms

Fill large mushroom caps each with a ball of spicy country sausage. Arrange on baking sheet and broil until sausage meat is done and mushroom caps are soft. Drain off grease while broiling.

Broiled Tomatoes

Cut tops from tomatoes. Wrap each tomato in two strips of bacon, crisscross. Broil in preheated broiler until bacon is crisp. Drain and serve hot.

Orange Blossom Biscuits

2 cups sifted flour
3 teaspoons baking powder
¾ teaspoon salt
2 tablespoons cold shortening
1 tablespoon grated orange rind
½ cup milk

¼ cup orange curaçao
Cube sugar
4 tablespoons orange-flower
    water
Confectioners' sugar

Sift flour, baking powder, and salt together and cut in shortening. Add orange rind and milk. Add orange curaçao. Stir quickly and knead lightly for a few seconds, using as little flour on board as possible. Roll out dough to ½-inch thickness and cut with floured cutter.

Put biscuit rounds together in pairs, with a cube of sugar moistened with orange-flower water between. Place on greased baking sheet and spread tops with confectioners' sugar moistened with orange curaçao. Bake in very hot oven at 450 degrees for 15 minutes. *(Makes about 18 two-inch biscuits.)*

Macaroon Mousse

18 macaroons	⅛ teaspoon salt
½ cup dark rum	2 tablespoons unflavored gelatin
5 egg yolks, beaten	¼ cup water
1 cup sugar	5 egg whites, stiffly beaten
3 cups milk	1 teaspoon vanilla extract

Line a pudding mold with macaroons and pour rum over them. In top of a double boiler, beat egg yolks with sugar. Add milk and salt. Cook custard, stirring constantly until it is thick and creamy. Soften gelatin in water and dissolve it in hot custard. Fold in egg whites and add vanilla. Pour custard over macaroons in mold and chill 3 hours, or until firm. Unmold mousse on a platter and serve with rum-flavored whipped cream. *(Makes 6 servings.)*

Silver Wedding Anniversary Dinner

LOVING CUP COCKTAIL
SPICED PEACH PUNCH
SILVER STALLION FIZZ

HOT OYSTER COCKTAIL

CHATEAUBRIAND A LA OLD HOUSE
LOVAGE POTATOES
ITALIAN BROAD BEANS WITH CARAWAY

MUSHROOM SALAD

SILVER CAKE
AFTER-DINNER BRANDIES
HONEY MEAT

Loving Cup Cocktail

2 lemons
½ teaspoon lemon balm
½ teaspoon borage
½ teaspoon ground cardamom
   seed

1 cup sugar
1 cup water
½ bottle Madeira
½ cup brandy
1 bottle good champagne

Grate lemons; peel off remaining white rind and slice lemons paper thin. Put balm, borage, cardamom, sliced lemons, lemon rind, and sugar into a large pitcher. Add water, Madeira, and brandy. Cover and chill in refrigerator for 1 hour. Chill champagne and, when ready to serve, add it to the other chilled ingredients. Stir and serve in champagne glasses. *(Makes 12 glasses.)*

Spiced Peach Punch

1 quart apple juice
6 whole cloves
1 stick cinnamon about 2 inches
  long
½ teaspoon costmary (available
  at gourmet shops and
  pharmacies)

1 teaspoon dried lemon balm
½ cup honey or ⅓ cup sugar
1 quart apricot nectar
1 quart ginger ale
Spiced peaches
Nutmeg

Put apple juice and spices with honey or sugar in a kettle and bring to a boil. Cool and store in refrigerator until needed. When ready to serve, pour spiced apple juice into a pitcher or punch bowl. Add apricot nectar and ginger ale. Stir and strain out spices. Slice spiced peaches very thin and float on top. Sprinkle all lightly with grated nutmeg. *(Makes 12 glasses.)*

Silver Stallion Fizz

1 scoop vanilla ice cream
¼ teaspoon grated crystallized
  ginger

2 ounces dry gin
Club soda

Put ice cream, ginger, and gin in 8-ounce highball glass, stir, and fill glass with soda.

Hot Oyster Cocktail

1 pint raw shucked oysters and
  their liquor
1 teaspoon grated lemon peel
¼ teaspoon mace
½ teaspoon ground coriander
  seed

½ cup tomato paste
¼ teaspoon sugar
¼ teaspoon salt
⅛ teaspoon coarsely ground
  black pepper
¼ cup drained horseradish

Drain liquor from oysters. (You should get about 1 cup.) Add rest of ingredients to oyster liquor and mix. Bring to a boil; add oysters and cook over medium heat just until the edges curl. Remove from heat, and stir in 2 tablespoons cream. Pour hot cocktail into sherbet cups or glasses and serve immediately with wedges of lemon. *(Makes 6 servings.)*

Châteaubriand à la Old House (Roast Filet of Beef)

1 whole, trimmed beef tenderloin

Wipe beef with a damp cloth. Cover with the following marinade and let stand at room temperature for 1 hour:

MARINADE:

1 large onion, chopped
2 tablespoons chopped parsley
2 teaspoons salt
1 teaspoon black pepper
4 juniper berries, crushed

½ teaspoon thyme
1 cup vinegar
2 cups dry white wine
½ cup olive oil

Turn meat from time to time in marinade. Roast in a moderate oven at 375 degrees for 25 to 30 minutes, depending on size of filet. Baste frequently with marinade. For rare meat, cook 10 minutes on each side. For medium, cook 15 minutes on each side, and for well-done, 20 minutes on each side. *(Makes 6 servings.)*

Make a sauce of the unused marinade by adding 2 tablespoons flour creamed with 2 tablespoons butter. Cook over medium heat until thickened to gravy consistency, stirring constantly. Take from heat and stir in 1 tablespoon caraway seeds. Pass sauce with meat.

Lovage Potatoes

24 small whole potatoes, peeled
  and cooked firm
2 teaspoons finely chopped
  lovage leaves
3 tablespoons potato flour
1 egg

1 teaspoon salt
¼ teaspoon coarsely ground
  black pepper
3 tablespoons bread crumbs
1 tablespoon olive oil
2 tablespoons butter

Put potatoes, lovage leaves, and potato flour in a paper bag and shake until potatoes are well coated. Drop egg in a bowl and beat well. Turn potatoes into bowl and coat with egg. Sprinkle potatoes with salt and pepper and roll in bread crumbs. Heat olive oil and butter in skillet. Saute potatoes until golden brown, turning often to brown on all sides. **Note:** Chopped celery leaves may be used for this recipe instead of lovage. *(Makes 6 servings.)*

Italian Broad Beans with Caraway

Caraway is mentioned in ancient Greek and Roman lore as an ingredient in love potions. It was believed to keep lovers faithful; in fact, it was fed to pet doves to keep them at home. Try it in the dishes for this Silver Wedding dinner — it may still work.

Place 3 packages (9 ounces each) frozen green Italian broad beans in salted water and cook a few minutes until tender. Do not overcook. Drain. Add 4 tablespoons minced dehydrated onion, 2 tablespoons butter, and 1 tablespoon caraway seeds. Toss lightly and serve immediately. *(Serves 6.)*

Mushroom Salad

3 pounds very large fresh mushrooms	1 tablespoon celery salt
½ cup olive oil	1 teaspoon fennel
3½ cups water	½ teaspoon thyme
Juice of 2 lemons, strained	1 large bay leaf
1 tablespoon chopped parsley	12 coriander seeds
	12 peppercorns

Wash mushrooms and slice from top through bottom of stems into ¼-inch-thick slices, being careful not to break off stems. In a saucepan mix rest of ingredients. Add sliced mushrooms. Bring to a boil and simmer mushrooms until they are tender. Let mushrooms cool in the seasoned water, then carefully lift them out, letting some of the spices cling to them. Heap lightly in lettuce cups and serve with French dressing. *(Makes 6 servings.)*

Silver Cake

3 cups sifted cake flour	2 cups sugar
3 teaspoons baking powder	1 teaspoon vanilla
½ teaspoon salt	1 cup milk
⅔ cup (1 stick plus 3 tablespoons) butter	5 egg whites

Sift flour, baking powder, and salt together. Cream butter with sugar and vanilla until fluffy. Add sifted dry ingredients and milk alternately in small amounts, beating well after each addition. Beat egg whites until stiff but not dry and fold into batter. Pour into 3 greased 9-inch pans and bake at 350 degrees for 30 minutes. *(Makes 3 layers.)*

FROSTING:

2 cups heavy cream	2 cups grated coconut
1½ teaspoons vanilla	
6 tablespoons confectioners' sugar, sifted	

Whip cream until peaks form. Add vanilla and fold in sugar. Spread between layers and over top of cake. Sprinkle coconut between layers and over top. Finally, sprinkle top and sides of cake with decorator silver confections. The silver particles with the shredded coconut make a beautiful cake.

After-Dinner Brandies

You need a wide-mouthed glass or ceramic jug to make this drink in. Cover jug with several layers of cheesecloth, but *do not cork*, and do not entirely fill.

1 tablespoon aniseed	1 teaspoon mace
1 teaspoon sweet fennel seeds	1 pound raisins
1 tablespoon green licorice	½ pound figs
(available at gourmet shops	1 slice licorice root
or pharmacies)	1 gallon good brandy
1 teaspoon coriander seed	1 teaspoon saffron
1 teaspoon cloves	

Bruise all the spices and fruit except saffron and infuse in the brandy for 8 days. Then strain and stir in saffron and leave for 2 more days. Stir from time to time during the 10 days. The brandy is then ready to drink.

This brandy will have a wonderful aroma and should be served in brandy snifters filled only ¼ full. Warm the brandy snifters first.

Honey Meat

Here is the *pièce de résistance* for all midnight icebox raiders! It will give you a wonderful well-filled feeling, with none of the bad dreams that usually follow the beer, cheese, and icebox leftovers. Also, the royal honey of the queen bee has been noted for centuries for its great rejuvenating powers.

Cut whatever kind of bread you prefer into a hot bowl (as for bread and milk). Add 1 or 2 tablespoons of queen bee royal honey and enough cider to soak all thoroughly. Fill with hot milk — as hot as you can stand it — and eat in bed.

Golden Wedding Anniversary Buffet

GOLDEN GLOW PUNCH

CHICKEN D'OR

GOLDEN BANTAM CORN AND CHEDDAR PUDDING
GOLDEN CURRIED FRUIT
GOLDEN BEAN SALAD

APPLE LEMON CHIFFON PIE
GOLDEN WEDDING CAKE

Golden Glow Punch

1 fifth orange gin
1 cup light rum

3 large bottles 7-Up

Combine liquors, float ice in bowl, and add 7-Up just before serving.

Chicken d'Or

50 chicken breasts
7 quarts plus 1 cup chicken broth, bouillon, or stock
¾ pound (3 sticks) butter or margarine
3 cups flour
2 tablespoons salt
1½ tablespoons coarsely ground black pepper
2 quarts light cream
1¾ cups chopped onions

2½ cups chopped red pimiento
2½ cups chopped parsley
2½ cups diced celery
1 gallon (25 cups) cooked long-grain and wild-rice blend
2 cups almonds, blanched and chopped
2 level teaspoons saffron
4 large bay leaves
2 cups dry sherry

Bone and skin chicken breasts. Poach in 25 cups broth (6 quarts plus 1 cup) until tender. Cut meat into 1-inch cubes.

Cream 2 sticks butter, flour, salt, and pepper until smooth. Over low heat stir in cream and remaining 1 quart chicken broth. Melt 1 stick butter, saute onion, pimiento, parsley, and celery.

Combine all ingredients except sherry and mix well. Pour into greased pan. Bake at 425 degrees for 1 hour. Stir in sherry just before serving. *(Makes 50 servings.)*

Golden Bantam Corn and Cheddar Pudding

2 tablespoons dry mustard	3 pounds grated cheddar cheese
2 tablespoons water	2 quarts soft bread crumbs
1 pound butter or margarine	3 tablespoons salt
2 cups flour	2 tablespoons sugar
3 quarts milk	2 teaspoons coarsely ground
3 packages (5 pounds each)	black pepper
frozen whole-kernel corn	2 dozen eggs

Combine mustard and water. Let stand 10 minutes for flavor to develop. Melt butter; blend in flour. Gradually stir in milk over low heat and cook, stirring until thickened and smooth. Remove from heat. Add mustard and remaining ingredients; mix well. Turn into buttered baking pans. Bake over hot water at 325 degrees 1¼ hours, or until a knife inserted in center comes out clean. *(Makes 50 servings.)*

Golden Curried Fruit

2 quarts canned mandarin orange sections, drained	¾ cup curry powder
	1½ pounds butter, melted
50 canned pear halves, drained	Juice from drained mandarin
50 canned cling peach halves, drained	oranges, plus enough orange juice to make 1½ quarts
50 canned pineapple slices, drained	1½ quarts blanched slivered almonds
1 pound dark brown sugar	

Arrange fruits in casserole. Mix brown sugar, curry powder, melted butter, and orange juice. Pour over fruits. Sprinkle with almonds. Bake at 350 degrees for 20 minutes.

Golden Bean Salad

1 gallon canned pineapple
    chunks
2 gallons yellow wax beans,
    cooked and drained (canned
    are good)
1 gallon mild pickled yellow
    peppers, coarsely chopped
1 quart diced celery
¼ cup cornstarch
¼ cup dry mustard
2 teaspoons pepper
2 teaspoons chopped dill
3 tablespoons sugar
4 teaspoons seasoned salt
1 cup wine vinegar
2 cups pineapple syrup (drained
    from canned pineapple
    chunks)
1 cup olive oil

Drain pineapple, reserving required amount of syrup. Drain beans and peppers. Combine pineapple and vegetables, cover, and chill. Mix cornstarch and seasonings, blend with vinegar, and add pineapple syrup. Cook and stir over moderate heat until thickened. Remove from heat; beat in olive oil. Toss vegetables and pineapple with dressing, mixing well. Chill. *(Makes 50 servings.)*

Apple Lemon Chiffon Pie

3 quarts (about 6 cans) canned
    spiced apple pie filling
9 baked pie shells (9-inch size)
1-pound package lemon chiffon
    pie filling mix

Put spiced apple pie filling into each shell. Prepare lemon chiffon pie filling as directed on package. Top each pie with 7½ ounces of lemon chiffon filling. Refrigerate 2 hours or longer. *(Makes nine 9-inch pies.)*

Golden Wedding Cake

3 cups sifted cake flour
3 teaspoons baking powder
¼ teaspoon salt
⅔ cup (1 stick plus 3
    tablespoons) butter
1½ cups sugar
1 teaspoon vanilla extract
3 eggs, separated, yolks and
    whites well beaten
1 cup milk

Sift together flour, baking powder, and salt. Cream butter until soft and gradually add sugar, beating constantly. Beat in vanilla extract and well-beaten egg yolks. Gradually add dry ingredients, alternately with milk, beating well after each addition. Fold in stiffly beaten egg whites. Pour batter into 4 buttered round layer-cake tins, graduated in size from 3 to 9 inches, and bake in moderate oven for 20 to 25 minutes, or until a broom straw inserted in middle of cake comes out clean. Cool cakes and put together with Lemon Frosting.

Lemon Frosting

2 egg whites, unbeaten **Pinch of salt**
1 cup sugar **⅔ cup lemon juice**

Combine first 3 ingredients in top of double boiler. Beat 1 minute with electric mixer or hand beater, adding lemon juice gradually. Place over boiling water; beat constantly until frosting forms peaks, about 7 minutes. Remove from boiling water. Beat until of spreading consistency, about 2 or 3 minutes.

Christening

GRASSHOPPER PUNCH
ORANGE SPARKLE

ASSORTED TINY FANCY SANDWICHES

LEMON CREAM PUFFS
NUT OR COCONUT TOASTIES
SPICED NUTS
CHOCOLATE RUM BALLS
PORCUPINES

Grasshopper Punch

½ pint Triple Sec or other
    orange-flavored liqueur
1 pint crème de cacao (white)
1 pint green crème de menthe

1 quart club soda
Confectioners' sugar to taste
2 quarts champagne

Place large block of ice in punch bowl with liqueurs, soda, and sugar, and mix well. Add champagne. Float paper-thin slices of lime on top. *(Makes 30 punch cups.)*

Orange Sparkle

1 fifth of champagne, well
    chilled

Equal amount of orange juice,
    well chilled

Pour orange juice first into glass until half filled. Fill with cold champagne. Do not use ice.

Assorted Tiny Fancy Sandwiches

Fill sandwiches before cutting. Use tin cookie cutters of all shapes and small sizes to cut out sandwiches. Space cookie cutters so that remaining parts of sandwiches are large enough, with intriguing shapes, to be used also. Heap sandwiches on a serving tray. Rub a little water on the inside of a plastic bag large enough to cover the entire tray. Enclose tray in the damp plastic and seal. The sandwiches will stay soft and fresh indefinitely, until needed.

Trim crusts from bread and slice thinly. Spread a very thin layer of soft butter on one side of each slice. This will keep the filling from making the bread soggy. Put filling between the two buttered sides. For interesting variety of textures and colors, use several of the following breads:

White bread	**Raisin bread**
Whole wheat bread	**Oatmeal bread**
Canned date-nut bread cut into thin rounds	**Cheese bread**
	Rye bread
Cinnamon bread	**Pumpernickel**
Orange bread, canned, cut into rounds	**Egg bread (pale yellow is lovely)**

Fillings:

2 cups ground cooked tongue, 1 cup ground Brazil nuts, 1 cup chopped black olives. Enough mayonnaise to bind. Season with salt to taste.

6 ounces soft cream cheese, 3 tablespoons mayonnaise, 1½ teaspoons prepared mustard, ¾ teaspoon sugar.

4-ounce tin of smoked oysters, drained on paper and chopped finely. Mix with 4 tablespoons butter, ½ teaspoon lemon juice, ¼ teaspoon finely grated lemon rind.

½ pound cooked shrimps, chopped, ½ cup mayonnaise, 2 small spring onions, minced, including tops, 1 tablespoon capers. Salt and pepper to taste.

2 hard-cooked eggs, 1 bunch of radishes, 4 spring onions with tops, ½ cup watercress leaves, ½ cucumber, peeled and seeded. Chop all. Mix with ½ cup mayonnaise and 1 teaspoon prepared mustard.

4 ounces cream cheese, 2 tablespoons sour cream, 6 ounces red caviar.

1 cup finely diced cooked chicken, ¼ pound cooked mushrooms, 3 hard-cooked eggs, 1 tablespoon dill, all chopped. Mix with 4 tablespoons sour cream, salt and pepper to taste.

1½ cups chopped cooked ham, ½ cup chopped green onions with tops, 1 teaspoon grated horseradish, ½ teaspoon sweet mustard, 1 cup whipped cream.

1 pound cooked shrimps, finely chopped, 3 tablespoons chutney, 3 tablespoons chopped preserved ginger, 2 teaspoons curry powder, 3 ounces cream cheese, 4 tablespoons sour cream.

8 slices liverwurst, 2 hard-cooked eggs, 4 tablespoons grated Swiss cheese, 1 teaspoon Worcestershire sauce, 1 teaspoon prepared mustard, 1 teaspoon grated onion. Enough mayonnaise to bind.

½ pound grated Swiss cheese, ¼ pound soft butter, ½ teaspoon prepared sweet mustard, ½ cup chopped pistachio nuts.

½ cup grated American cheese, ¼ cup crumbled crisp bacon, 6 drops onion juice, 1 tablespoon minced sweet pickle, 3 tablespoons mayonnaise.

1 cup ground cooked chicken, ½ cup minced celery, ¼ cup ground almonds, ¼ cup mayonnaise.

1½ cups cooked crabmeat, ¾ cup minced celery, 1 tablespoon minced pimiento, 1 tablespoon minced green pepper, ¼ teaspoon salt. Enough mayonnaise to bind.

Lemon Cream Puffs

Tiny cream puff shells (from bakery)

LEMON FILLING:

4 egg yolks	2 tablespoons butter
1 cup sugar	1 teaspoon grated lemon rind
1 teaspoon cornstarch	¼ cup lemon juice

Beat egg yolks. Mix sugar and cornstarch very thoroughly and add to egg yolks. Add butter, lemon rind, and juice, and cook over hot water, stirring frequently until very thick. Make a small hole in cream puff shells and force filling into shells with a pastry tube. The cream puffs should only be about 1 or 1½ inches in diameter. *(Makes filling for 2 dozen 1-inch puffs.)*

Nut or Coconut Toasties

4 slices bread 1-inch thick	1 teaspoon sugar
1 egg, beaten	1 cup finely chopped nuts or
¼ cup milk	finely chopped coconut, or
½ teaspoon salt	½ cup each

Remove crusts from bread, and cut each slice into strips 1 inch wide. Beat egg, add milk, salt, and sugar, and dip bread in batter. Roll in nuts or coconut and fry in hot deep fat at 385 degrees until brown, or bake in a hot oven at 450 degrees for 15 minutes. *(Makes 1 dozen toasties.)*

Spiced Nuts

2 cups sugar
2 teaspoons salt
1 teaspoon ground nutmeg
3 tablespoons ground cinnamon
2 teaspoons ground ginger

1 tablespoon ground cloves
2 egg whites
2 cups walnut halves, almonds,
  pecan halves (unsalted)

Sift sugar, salt, and spices together 3 times. Beat egg whites slightly with 2 tablespoons cold water. Put nuts in a wire strainer and dip them in egg and water mixture until each nut is well coated. Roll nuts in spiced sugar.

Spread a layer of spiced sugar on a baking sheet, spread nuts covered with sugar on top, cover with more spiced sugar, and bake at 300 degrees for 2 hours. Remove nuts from sugar. The balance of the sugar may be kept for another time, in a tightly closed jar.

Chocolate Rum Balls

1 cup vanilla wafer crumbs
Powdered mixture composed of
  1 teaspoon cocoa and ½
  teaspoon cinnamon to every
  rounded tablespoon of sifted
  confectioners' sugar

1 cup ground pecans, almonds,
  or walnuts
2 tablespoons cocoa
2 tablespoons white corn syrup
¼ cup Jamaica rum

Mix cookie crumbs with ground nuts, then add cocoa, corn syrup, and rum. Knead well. Mold dough into balls, 1 teaspoonful at a time. Roll in cocoa-cinnamon-sugar mixture. Place balls on baking sheet for 3 hours to dry. Roll once more in plain confectioners' sugar. *(Makes about 20 balls.)*

Porcupines

2 cups pecans
1 cup dates
2 cups shredded coconut

1 cup brown sugar
2 eggs, unbeaten

Grind pecans and dates in food chopper or blender. Mix in 1½ cups coconut and remaining ingredients. Scoop up spoonful of mixture and shape into roll ½-inch thick and 4 inches long. Roll each porcupine in remaining coconut. Place on greased baking sheet and bake 10 minutes at 350 degrees. *(Makes 40 porcupines.)*

Bar Mitzvah

HOT SPICED WINE
STRAWBERRY PUNCH

ROLLED LIVER CANAPE
DILLED MIXED VEGETABLES

APPLE PICKLE
RED SEA DIP
GARBANZO SPREAD
LIMED FISH

FILLED POTATO CROUSTADES
PICKLED CHERRIES
SPICED EGGS

THE SWEET TABLE: STRUDEL
APPLE
DRIED FRUIT
CHERRY
HONEY
AMBROSIA
SPONGE CAKE
ALMOND ROCK
CANDIED CHESTNUTS
PINEAPPLE SNOW CANDY
CHOCOLATE PRALINES
GLAZED APPLES
ORANGE BISCUITS

❊ Bar Mitzvah

It is an old Jewish belief that, at thirteen, a boy becomes a religious adult and from then on is responsible himself for carrying out the commandments of the faith. When my great-grandfather was a child, it was already an old tradition to mark a boy's Bar Mitzvah in some special way during a synagogue service, and also to have a family celebration. Since the Bar Mitzvah is, after all, a *simcha* (happy occasion), it is customary to have a joyous celebration after the worship service. However, the social party should not overshadow the spiritual import of the occasion.

Hot Spiced Wine

1 quart Mogen David wine	8 sticks cinnamon 1 inch long
2 oranges, sliced thin with peel	12 whole cloves
2 lemons, sliced thin with peel	

Mix ingredients while wine is cold, then heat wine to a point just below boiling, and serve in pottery wine mugs. *(Makes about 6 servings.)*

Strawberry Punch

1 quart fresh strawberries, sliced very thin	1 bottle sauterne
	1 cup cognac
½ cup sugar	4 bottles sparkling Burgundy

In a bowl, pour over sliced strawberries all ingredients but the Burgundy and let them marinate in refrigerator for at least 1 hour. At serving time, pour strawberry mixture over a block of ice in a punch bowl and slowly add sparkling Burgundy. Stir punch gently until well mixed and berry slices are floating on top. Paper-thin slices of lemon floated on top also add to the appearance. *(Makes 6 to 8 punch cups.)*

Rolled Liver Canapé

1 cup cooked ground chicken
  livers
3 tablespoons chicken fat
1 teaspoon grated onion
2 hard-cooked eggs, chopped

½ teaspoon salt
⅛ teaspoon ground pepper
1 teaspoon chopped stuffed
  olives

Mix all ingredients to a paste. If necessary, add a little more chicken fat to spread easily. Cut crust from thinly sliced brown bread, spread with liver paste, roll up, fasten with a toothpick, and bake in a very hot oven 5 minutes until browned on all sides.

Dilled Mixed Vegetables

For this dish you will want several vegetables such as asparagus, cauliflowerettes, celery hearts, broccoli, leeks, carrots, whole long green beans, and whole okra pods, cooked until tender but not overcooked. Cut carrots into strips; cut leeks in half. Marinate vegetables for at least 2 hours in:

½ cup chopped dill
½ cup salad oil
½ cup wine vinegar
1 teaspoon salt
1 teaspoon dry mustard

½ teaspoon coarsely ground
  fresh black pepper
1 clove garlic, pressed or
  mashed

To serve, remove from marinade and arrange on a tray, keeping each vegetable in a mound to itself. Garnish between mounds with parsley. Sprinkle vegetables lavishly with more chopped dill.

Apple Pickle

Take equal quantities of sliced raw onion, sliced cucumber, and sliced unpeeled sour apples, plus salt and pepper to taste. To 1 cup cider vinegar, add ½ cup each dry sherry and soy sauce. Pour over apple mixture. Let stand for a few hours before serving.

Red Sea Dip

1 pint mashed ripe avocado pulp
½ pound red caviar
½ cup minced onion

1 tablespoon Worcestershire
  sauce

Mash avocado with a silver fork (to prevent discoloring). Mix all ingredients and serve with wafers.

Garbanzo Spread

6 cups canned garbanzo beans, drained

1 cup chopped onions

½ cup pine nuts, ground or chopped fine

½ cup sesame seeds

Mash beans and liquid together with 1 teaspoon salt. Mix with rest of ingredients. Serve with crisp wafers.

Limed Fish

This is the oldest known method of preparing fish. The fish is actually raw, but it doesn't taste raw, and you'll find it delicious.

Thaw frozen fillet of halibut and cut into 1-inch squares. Put squares in a pan and cover completely with fresh lime juice. Refrigerate for 4 hours. To serve, rinse in cold water. Arrange sprinkled with a little black pepper. The fish comes out firm and white, as though cooked, and is wonderfully flavored.

Filled Potato Croustades

Pare 6 large Idaho potatoes and cut into long thin strips. Cook in deep hot oil until potatoes are soft but not colored, about 5 minutes. Remove from hot oil and drain. While soft and limp, interlace the strips in a basket-weave design and press them into well-oiled muffin tins or ramekins. Bake until browned. Remove from tins, sprinkle with a little salt, and fill with the following.

FILLING:

¼ cup (½ stick) margarine

1½ cups water

3 level tablespoons dry mustard

¼ cup 57 Sauce

¾ teaspoon sugar

½ teaspoon salt

¼ teaspoon coarsely ground black pepper

1½ cups hollandaise sauce

Juice of 1 lemon

1½ pounds (3 heaping cups) flaked canned red salmon

Combine all ingredients except salmon and cook over hot water, stirring sauce until smooth and thick. Add salmon to sauce, mix well, and pour into potato shells. *(Makes 12 croustades.)*

Pickled Cherries

You will need 1 quart cherries (black or yellow) with stems, as fresh and as large as you can get them. Put cherries in a glass jar. Sprinkle with chopped thyme and chopped bay leaf. Bring to a boil 2 cups cider vinegar, 1 teaspoon salt, and ½ teaspoon whole cloves. Pour over cherries. Put a lid on the jar but do not tighten. Let cherries stand 2 weeks. They will be crisp and excellent to garnish or decorate with, or simply to pile in a bowl to eat.

Spiced Eggs

16 hard-cooked eggs
1 tablespoon black peppercorns
1 tablespoon allspice

1 tablespoon ginger
4 cups cider vinegar

Remove eggshells and arrange eggs compactly in a wide-necked jar. Boil peppercorns, allspice, and ginger in vinegar until some of their flavor is extracted, and pour while boiling hot over the eggs. Cool, cover tightly, and store in refrigerator for at least 1 hour before serving. May be served plain or stuffed.

Strudel
Stretched Strudel Dough

3 cups sifted flour
¼ teaspoon salt
2 eggs

3 tablespoons oil
¼ cup lukewarm water

Sift flour and salt into a bowl. Make a well in the center and drop in eggs, oil, and water. Work into flour, mixing until dough leaves sides of bowl. Knead dough for 10 minutes, or until smooth and elastic. Cover and put in warm place for 20 minutes.

Use a working surface large enough for strudel to be stretched on, but one that you can walk around. A center kitchen table is fine. Cover table with a cloth, and dust cloth well with flour. Roll out dough as thin as you can, then begin stretching it. Flour your hands and gently pull dough toward you from underneath. Work around table as you stretch dough so that no one part of it will be stretched too thin. Stretch until dough is transparent, then brush with melted butter. Do not have any thick edges.

Spread with any of the following fillings and roll up. Brush with melted butter. Bake in a 400-degree oven on heavily greased baking sheet for 35 minutes, or until strudel is brown and crisp. Cut into thick slices immediately after taking from oven. *(Makes 35 to 40 slices.)*

Apple Filling

1 cup fine bread crumbs
1½ cups ground almonds
4 cups chopped apples
2 tablespoons grated lemon rind

2 tablespoons lemon juice
1 cup sultanas
½ cup sugar mixed with
   2 teaspoons cinnamon

Sprinkle bread crumbs over half the oiled, stretched dough. Sprinkle nuts over it and spread evenly with your hand. Mix apples, lemon rind, lemon juice, and sultanas together. Spread over nuts, sprinkle with sugar-cinnamon mixture. Roll up and bake.

Dried Fruit Filling

1 pound prunes, pitted
1 pound dates, pitted
½ cup chopped maraschino
   cherries
½ cup chopped candied lemon,
   orange, or grapefruit peel

1 whole lemon
2 cups walnuts
4 tablespoons sugar
2 teaspoons cinnamon
1 teaspoon nutmeg

Chop all ingredients very fine except sugar, cinnamon, and nutmeg. Mix well. Spread on oiled strudel dough, sprinkle on sugar and spices, roll up, brush with melted butter, and bake.

Cherry Filling

1½ cups pistachio nuts
1 cup sugar

4 cups drained pitted black
   cherries

Spread nuts over oiled dough, cover with cherries and sugar, roll up, brush with melted butter, and bake.

Honey Filling

1 cup honey
½ cup cream
1 pound poppy seeds (2½ cups)

½ cup chopped almonds
1 tablespoon grated lemon rind
3 tablespoons melted butter

Cook honey, cream, poppy seeds, and almonds until thick. Do not boil or cream will curdle. Stir in lemon rind and cool. Spread on oiled strudel dough and roll up. Brush with butter. Bake until browned and crisp.

Ambrosia Filling

2 cups shredded coconut	1 cup orange marmalade
2 cups chopped nuts	1 cup gooseberry preserves

Mix coconut, nuts, marmalade, and preserves together. Spread on oiled dough, roll up, and bake.

Sponge Cake

6 eggs, separated	¾ teaspoon vanilla
1¼ cups sugar	¼ teaspoon salt
2 teaspoons lemon juice	1½ cups sifted cake flour
1 teaspoon grated lemon rind	

Beat egg yolks until light and lemon-colored. Add sugar very slowly, beating constantly. Beat at least 10 minutes, then add 3 tablespoons cold water, stirring constantly. Stir in lemon juice, lemon rind, and vanilla. Beat egg whites with salt until stiff but not dry. Put beaten egg whites on top of yolk mixture.

Sift cake flour into egg mixture. Do not stir but carefully cut and fold in egg mixture and flour. Pour batter into an unbuttered 9-inch tube pan, and bake at 300 degrees for 1 hour without opening oven door.

When cake is done, cool it in the pan, upside down. If cake has risen above sides of pan, which it may do, turn pan upside down and support it on the edges of cups. When the cake is perfectly cold, loosen sides with a spatula if necessary.

Almond Rock

5 ounces almonds (1½ cups)	1 cup glucose
1 pound moist brown sugar	Almond extract
½ cup water	

Blanch almonds, split them in halves lengthwise, and place, cut side down, on an oiled or buttered baking sheet. Dissolve sugar in water and glucose, and boil to 312 degrees using a large stewpan, as mixture is apt to boil over. Let preparation cool slightly, then add ½ teaspoon almond extract. Pour slowly over almonds. Allow to harden.

Candied Chestnuts

Remove shells of chestnuts, place them in a stewpan of boiling water, and boil for 10 minutes. Drain and skin them. Replace in stewpan, cover with boiling water, and boil until tender but not broken. Let cool.

Allow 1 cup water to each pound sugar and boil to 290 degrees, then dip in chestnuts one at a time, and place them on an oiled sheet to cool.

Pineapple Snow Candy

2 cups white corn syrup
1 egg white
1 tablespoon sugar

½ teaspoon or more pineapple extract

Boil syrup to 290 degrees and plunge pan into cold water to stop the cooking. Let cool. Beat egg white stiffly, and add sugar and pineapple flavoring. Line some molds or tins with oiled paper and sprinkle bottoms and sides liberally with confectioners' sugar. Pour cooled syrup on stiff egg white and sugar, and stir to a froth. Pour into prepared molds and turn out when set.

Chocolate Pralines

2 cups chopped and blanched almonds
4 cups seeded raisins

1 teaspoon almond extract
2 pound bars bitter chocolate, melted

Mix nuts, raisins, and almond extract, and put through food chopper. Roll mixture into small balls and allow them to dry. Press flat before drying. Dip in melted chocolate and place on a baking sheet to cool and harden.

Glazed Apples

SYRUP FOR GLAZING:

6 pounds sugar
5 cups water

1 egg white

Dissolve sugar in 4 cups water in a stewpan, but do not let it become very hot. Beat egg white, pour warm syrup on it, and return to stewpan. When syrup boils, add ⅓ cup cold water. Bring to boil again. Repeat 3 times, using in all 1 cup cold water. Cool.

10 to 12 small apples of equal size	**Syrup**
Sugar	**Apricot jam**
Lemon juice	**Currant jelly**
	Crystallized angelica

Pare and core apples and simmer them very gently in water to which sugar to taste and a little lemon juice have been added. Drain apples well, pour over them a little syrup, and cover tightly. When cold, coat the apples with apricot jam, fill cavities with currant jelly, and decorate with crystallized angelica.

Orange Biscuits

2 cups sifted flour	**1 tablespoon grated orange rind**
3 teaspoons baking powder	**½ cup orange curaçao**
¾ teaspoon salt	**¾ cup milk**
2 tablespoons cold shortening	

Sift flour, baking powder, and salt together. Cut in shortening. Add orange rind, orange curaçao, and milk. Stir quickly and knead lightly. Roll out to ½-inch thickness and cut with floured cutter.

Put biscuits together as sandwiches, with ½ teaspoon orange marmalade between two rounds. Place on greased baking sheet and dust tops with confectioners' sugar. Bake at 450 degrees for 15 minutes. *(Makes eighteen 2-inch biscuits.)*

Fourth of July Patio Party

LIBERTY COCKTAIL
STARS AND STRIPES
GUIDED MISSILE

BARBECUED CHICKEN AND HAM STEAKS
ASH-ROASTED POTATOES AND ONIONS
BARBECUED TOMATOES WITH DILL

CHARCOAL-GRILLED BANANAS

Liberty Cocktail

¾ ounce imported rum   ¼ teaspoon simple sugar syrup
1½ ounces applejack

Stir with cracked ice and strain into cocktail glass.

Stars and Stripes

⅓ grenadine
⅓ white crème de menthe
⅓ Crème Yvette

Pour carefully, in order given, into pony glass so that each ingredient floats on the preceding one. Hurrah for the Red, White, and Blue! This is not only a delicious drink but a beautiful one.

Guided Missile

1½ ounces bourbon whiskey
½ ounce brandy
Dash bitters

¼ teaspoon Triple Sec or other orange-flavored liqueur
¼ teaspoon confectioners' sugar

Stir well with cracked ice and strain into cocktail glass. Add a twist of lemon peel.

Barbecued Chicken and Ham Steaks

3 broiler-fryers (2 pounds each)
3 smoked ham steaks (¼-inch thick)

Salt
Coarsely ground black pepper

MARINADE FOR CHICKENS:

1 cup olive oil
1 cup port wine

Juice of 1 lemon

MARINADE FOR HAM STEAKS:

1 cup olive oil
¼ cup lemon juice
1 tablespoon Worcestershire sauce

1 tablespoon dry mustard
1 clove garlic, mashed
1 bay leaf, crushed

Cut chickens in half and break joints so that halves will lie flat in a pan. Cover chickens with marinade and let stand for several hours, turning them over from time to time.

Place ham steaks in a shallow pan, cover with marinade, and marinate several hours, turning from time to time.

Sprinkle chickens generously with salt and pepper. Place on charcoal grill and baste frequently with remaining marinade while cooking. Turn to cook on all sides. Cook ham steaks slowly also, basting with marinade and turning to brown nicely on both sides.

Serve each half-chicken on a half-ham steak. *(Makes 6 servings).*

Ash-Roasted Potatoes and Onions

Scrub medium-sized baking potatoes. Peel medium-sized Bermuda or red Italian onions. Dip both in water, sprinkle well with salt and pepper, and while still wet wrap together in pairs in aluminum foil. Bury potatoes and

118

onions in hot coals for 40 minutes, or until they are soft when pricked with a fork. To serve, fold back foil, split and squash potato, and serve with a blob of butter on top of both potato and onion.

Barbecued Tomatoes with Dill

Cut large firm tomatoes in half. Brush with smoky barbecue sauce and place, cut side down, on side of grill away from intense heat. Cook tomatoes about 3 minutes, depending on the fire. (Don't overcook or they will be difficult to turn.) Turn tomatoes over and prick with a fork. Sprinkle cut surface with a little finely chopped dill and pour a little melted butter on each. Cook until tomato skin blisters.

Charcoal-Grilled Bananas

Use slightly green bananas. Lay unpeeled fruit on grill, turning with tongs. Cook for about 15 minutes. To serve, peel back one section of skin and sprinkle banana pulp with brown sugar, a little rum, and a bit of cinnamon. Serve in remaining peel with a spoon to scoop the banana out with.

Fourth of July
Picnic

RASPBERRY VINEGAR
THERMOS JUG CLARET LEMONADE
THERMOS JUG GINBUCKS
RED ANTS COCKTAIL IN A PAPER CUP

HAM TARTS
GREEK-AMERICAN POTATO SALAD
PATRIOTIC PEPPER CABBAGE
STONE JAR GARLIC TOMATOES

FRUITED RUM WATERMELON

Raspberry Vinegar

8 pints fresh raspberries	**Sugar**
2 cups vinegar	

Mash berries, add vinegar, and let stand for 4 days. To each cup of liquid add 1 cup sugar. Bring to a boil and cook for 20 minutes. Strain and bottle. May be used immediately or when needed. To serve, pour over ice cubes.

Thermos Jug Claret Lemonade

Juice of 12 lemons	**1 orange, sliced paper thin,**
1 cup sugar	**with seeds removed**
2 lemons, sliced paper thin,	**1 cup sliced cocktail cherries**
with seeds removed	**1 bottle good claret wine**

Put in gallon thermos jug and fill jug with ice cubes. Add enough water to bring liquid to brim.

Thermos Jug Ginbucks

Juice of 12 lemons
¼ cup sugar

1 quart dry gin
2 quarts ginger ale

Put in gallon thermos jug and fill jug to brim with ice cubes.

Red Ants Cocktail in a Paper Cup

Fill cup half full of cold tomato juice. Add 2 drops Worcestershire sauce, and salt and pepper to taste. Fill cup with cold beer. Sounds terrible, but it is really delicious!

Ham Tarts

Pastry for double 9-inch pie
  crust
4 cups diced cooked ham
1 cup cooked mushrooms
1 cup condensed celery soup
1 egg, beaten lightly
¼ cup diced cooked carrots

¼ cup diced cooked celery
¼ cup cooked peas
¼ cup dehydrated onion flakes
1 teaspoon salt
¼ teaspoon coarsely ground
  black pepper
⅛ teaspoon ground ginger

Roll out pastry and fit into eight 4-inch tart pans. Mix all ingredients and fill tarts. Cover tarts with pastry, pricking top to let steam escape. Bake in a hot oven (450 degrees) until crust is brown. Cool, remove from pans, and wrap each tart separately in a plastic sandwich bag. These are delicious cold. *(Makes 8 tarts.)*

Greek-American Potato Salad

6 large potatoes
1 cup chicken bouillon
2 tablespoons olive oil
1 tablespoon tarragon vinegar
2 cups white wine
½ teaspoon chervil

½ teaspoon chopped parsley
½ teaspoon marjoram
½ teaspoon salt
¼ teaspoon coarsely ground
  black pepper

Peel potatoes and boil them until done in chicken stock. Cool in stock. Remove and slice. Combine all other ingredients and pour over cold potato slices, mixing lightly. Refrigerate for at least 2 hours. *(Makes 6 servings.)*

Patriotic Pepper Cabbage

2 cups shredded cabbage (a
combination of red and white
cabbage makes a pretty dish)
1 green pepper, diced
1 red pepper, diced

1 teaspoon salt
½ teaspoon pepper
1 tablespoon celery seed
1 cup hot salad dressing

Pour the following hot dressing over all ingredients and mix well. Chill.
(Makes 6 servings.)

DRESSING:

1 tablespoon bacon fat or
drippings
1 teaspoon flour
½ cup vinegar
2 teaspoons sugar
½ teaspoon dry mustard

⅛ teaspoon pepper
½ teaspoon salt
1 egg yolk, beaten
1 cup crumbled crisp-fried
bacon

Melt bacon fat and blend in flour. Add vinegar and stir until mixture
thickens. Mix together sugar, mustard, salt, and pepper and add to liquid.
Cook for 4 minutes. Pour over beaten egg yolk, add bacon, and mix well.
Return to heat and cook 1 minute longer.

Stone Jar Garlic Tomatoes

*In the old days, stone jars or crocks were used for this sort of dish, but
today a glass quart jar will serve just as well.*

4 large tomatoes, cut in wedges
4 tablespoons olive oil
2 tablespoons tarragon vinegar
1 teaspoon coarsely ground
black pepper

1 teaspoon salt
1 tablespoon oregano
2 cloves garlic, mashed or
pressed

Put unpeeled tomato wedges in jar. Mix other ingredients and pour over
tomatoes. Invert jar two or three times gently, to mix everything well. Refrigerate overnight. *(Makes 6 servings.)*

Fruited Rum Watermelon

Cut a ripe, sweet watermelon in half lengthwise. Scoop out center and remove all seeds. Cut center part of melon into cubes. Mix watermelon cubes with pitted black canned cherries and pineapple cubes, and pile back into melon shell. Mound fruit up so that top half will fit tightly. Pour rum over fruit in lower half, until full. Replace top half of watermelon shell and seal all around with masking tape. Wrap melon in foil and turn over and over to rum-soak all the fruit. Pack in ice in a portable cooler. When ready to serve, unwrap melon, take off tape, and lift lid off carefully. Serve from shell onto paper dishes.

Labor Day Barbecue

FISH HOUSE PUNCH
SLOPPY JOE

CHARCOAL-BROILED BEEFBURGERS
BARBECUED ONIONS
GRILLED GREEN TOMATOES AND ZUCCHINI
ROAST CORN

GRILLED PEACHES

❋ Labor Day

On September 5, 1882, the Knights of Labor held a parade in New York City to honor the nation's wage earners. A few years later, Congress passed a bill designating the first Monday in September a national legal holiday. Canadians also celebrate Labor Day.

Fish House Punch

Juice of 1 dozen lemons
Enough confectioners' sugar to
  sweeten
1 quart club soda

1½ quarts brandy
1 pint peach-flavored brandy
1 pint imported dark rum

Pour lemon juice, sugar, and club soda over large block of ice in punch bowl and stir well. Add liquors. Stir well and decorate with thinly sliced fruits in season. Serve in punch cups. *(Makes 30 punch cups.)*

Sloppy Joe

¾ ounce pineapple juice
¾ ounce cognac
¾ ounce port wine

¼ teaspoon curaçao
¼ teaspoon grenadine

Shake with cracked ice and strain into cocktail glass.

Charcoal-Broiled Beefburgers

3 pounds coarsely ground chuck	2 tablespoons capers
1 cup soy sauce	2 tablespoons dehydrated onions
2 cloves garlic, crushed	2 tablespoons tomato ketchup
2 teaspoons grated ginger	

Mix all ingredients and shape into patties of desired size. Broil over hot coals, turning frequently. For those who like beef rare, put an ice cube in the center of the beefburgers before broiling. *(Makes 6 fat beefburgers.)*

Barbecued Onions

Peel large sweet onions. Sprinkle with black pepper, celery salt, marjoram, and grated cheese. Wrap onions in foil and bury in hot coals, roasting them for about 30 minutes.

Grilled Green Tomatoes and Zucchini

Slice green tomatoes ¼-inch thick. Cut zucchini in half lengthwise. Dip in the following marinade and broil 2 or 3 minutes on each side until tender.

MARINADE:

1 cup melted butter	½ teaspoon chopped sweet basil
1 clove garlic, minced	Salt and pepper

Baste tomato slices and zucchini while broiling.

Roast Corn

Open husk at top of each ear of corn and pull out silk. Sprinkle corn inside husk with salt, pepper, and melted butter. Sprinkle corn liberally with Beau Mond seasoning or celery salt. Wrap husk around ear of corn and dip quickly in and out of cold water. Roast ears over fairly hot coals about 15 minutes, turning to cook on all sides. Serve with additional melted butter to which chopped tarragon and chopped parsley have been added.

Grilled Peaches

Dip firm freestone peaches in boiling water and slip skins off. Break each in half and remove stone. Dip peach halves in grenadine and grill a few minutes, cavity sides up. Spoon grenadine over peach halves while cooking.

Rosh Hashanah
Dinner

GLAZED PINEAPPLE

GEFILTE FISH BALLS
WITH HORSERADISH AND BEETS

ROAST STUFFED TENDERLOIN OF BEEF
WITH APRICOT KIRSCH SAUCE

CUCUMBER AND ONION SALAD
BRUSSELS SPROUTS WITH CHESTNUTS
LATKES
RAM'S HORNS
ZABUD

MINTED ALMONDS

✳ *Rosh Hashanah*

One of the most important holidays in the Jewish religion is Rosh Hashanah, the Jewish New Year, or Feast of Trumpets. Sweet dishes are served to foretell a happy or sweet year.

Glazed Pineapple

Cut fresh ripe pineapples in half, leaving leaves or stem end on. Cut pineapple into cubes, leaving half-shells.

GLAZE:

1 cup water	¼ teaspoon cream of tartar
2 cups sugar	¼ teaspoon lemon juice

Boil water, sugar, and cream of tartar together over high heat until syrup begins to discolor and spin threads. Remove from heat and add lemon juice. Put pan into refrigerator or freezer compartment for a few minutes to stop boiling. Remove and place pan over hot water to prevent syrup from hardening. Dip cubes of pineapple, piece by piece, in syrup and place on wax paper to cool. When ready to serve, pile crystallized cubes back into half-shells. Fresh strawberries may be crystallized and used with the pineapple. This makes a beautiful dish.

Gefilte Fish Balls with Horseradish and Beets

¾ cup sugar	⅛ teaspoon pepper
2 teaspoons cornstarch	2 cups horseradish, drained
¼ cup vinegar	4 cups julienne beets (two
⅓ cup water	2½-pound cans, drained)
3 tablespoons margarine	1-pound jar gefilte-fish balls
¼ teaspoon salt	(gourmet shops carry them)

Combine sugar and cornstarch; add vinegar and water, and boil for 5 minutes. Add margarine and seasonings. Stir in horseradish and beets. Cook a few minutes until thickened. Heat gefilte-fish balls in own liquid. Drain and mix with beets and horseradish. *(Makes 6 to 8 servings.)*

Roast Stuffed Tenderloin of Beef

Trim completely all fat and sinew from a 5-pound whole beef tenderloin. Beginning at large end, make a large hole through entire length of tenderloin. (You can use a clean broomstick sharpened to a point.) Stuff cavity with pitted uncooked dried prunes and dried apricots. Sprinkle outside of tenderloin with salt and pepper. Wrap with twine to help keep its shape. Roast to desired doneness: 25 minutes for rare, 40 minutes for medium or pink. To serve, slice diagonally in 2-inch slices. Pour a small amount of Apricot Kirsch Sauce over slices. *(Makes 6 ample servings.)*

Apricot Kirsch Sauce

Dilute 1 cup apricot jam with 1 cup boiling water. Cream 1 tablespoon margarine with 1 tablespoon flour. Stir into hot apricot mixture. Stir constantly and cook until slightly thickened. Remove from fire and stir in 2 tablespoons kirsch. Pour over sliced meat.

Cucumber and Onion Salad

Peel large Bermuda onions and slice in rings 1/4-inch thick. Peel large cucumbers, quarter, and cut into pieces 1-inch long. Simmer onion rings and cucumber pieces in salted water until just transparent. Drain and cool. Serve mounded on greens with the following dressing:

Chop an onion and cook it in a little margarine, until just soft but not colored. Add a glass of Chablis, a large spoonful of consomme or meat drippings, the juice of a lemon, a bit of garlic, 1 chopped gherkin, 1 teaspoon capers, 1 tablespoon chopped parsley, 1 tablespoon chopped tarragon leaves, 1 clove, a pinch of nutmeg, and crushed peppercorns. Simmer 20 minutes and strain. When ready to serve, blend in a tablespoon of margarine and a tablespoon of chopped chervil and tarragon. *(Makes 6 servings.)*

Brussels Sprouts with Chestnuts

1/2 pound (1 cup) chestnuts	2 tablespoons margarine
1 pound (3 cups) fresh Brussels sprouts, cooked	Salt

Slit chestnuts on the round side. Put them in a pan with a little water, and roast in oven for 8 minutes. Peel them while they are still hot. After chestnuts are peeled, simmer them in salted water until tender. Boil Brussels sprouts rapidly in salted water. Do not overcook or they will loose their color; 10 to 15 minutes is usually enough. Drain. Mix with drained chestnuts and lightly saute them in the margarine. Sprinkle with a little seasoned salt and serve. *(Makes 6 servings.)*

Latkes *(Potato pancakes)*

6 medium potatoes	2 tablespoons grated onion
2 eggs, beaten	1 tablespoon chopped parsley
1/2 teaspoon salt	Matzo crumbs rolled very fine
1/4 teaspoon pepper	Margarine

Grate raw potatoes and drain off all liquid. Mix grated potatoes with eggs, salt, pepper, grated onion, and parsley. Add enough matzo crumbs to form into cakes. Fry in hot margarine until browned on both sides and crisp. Drain on paper and keep hot in oven. *(Makes 6 servings.)*

Ram's Horns

1 cake yeast
2 teaspoons sugar
1¼ cups lukewarm water
4½ cups sifted flour
2 teaspoons salt

2 eggs
2 tablespoons corn oil
1 egg yolk
4 tablespoons poppy seeds
Brown sugar

Combine yeast, sugar, and ¼-cup lukewarm water. Let stand 5 minutes. Sift flour and salt together. In center, drop eggs, oil, remaining water, and yeast mixture. Work into flour. Knead on a floured surface until smooth and elastic. Place in a bowl and brush top with a little oil. Cover, set in a warm place, and let rise 1 hour. Punch down, cover, and let rise until double in bulk.

Toss on a floured board, pat, and roll out ½-inch thick. Cut into 4-inch squares. Brush with egg yolk and sprinkle with poppy seeds. Roll each square from corner to corner to make a loose horn. Brush with oil, sprinkle with more poppy seeds and a little brown sugar. Cover and let horns rise 1 hour.

Bake at 450 degrees for 20 minutes or until brown and glazed. *(Makes 3 dozen horns.)*

Zabud

4-ounce can shredded coconut
1 cup cold (leftover) mashed
  potatoes

1 teaspoon almond extract
3 boxes (1 pound each)
  confectioners' sugar

Chop coconut fine. Mix with potatoes and almond extract, then gradually mix in sugar a little at a time. Shape into small balls by rolling between your hands. Roll in additional coconut and cinnamon.

Minted Almonds

1 cup sugar
½ cup water
1 tablespoon light corn syrup
1 pinch salt

6 marshmallows
½ teaspoon peppermint extract
3 cups almonds

Mix sugar, water, corn syrup, and salt in a saucepan and cook slowly for about 10 minutes. Just before it forms a soft ball when a little is dropped in cold water, remove from heat. Add marshmallows and stir until melted. Add peppermint extract and nuts, and stir until every nut is coated and mixture hardens. Cool on unglazed paper. These will keep well in the refrigerator.

Halloween Buffet

CAULDRON SMOKE
APPLEJACK COCKTAIL
CIDER CUP

SARDINE APPLES
ROQUEFORT APPLES
BROILED CHUTNEY PRUNES
CURRIED ALMONDS AND WALNUTS
CAT TOASTS
STUFFED PUMPKINS
HOT PUSSYCATS
LETTUCE ROSETTE SALAD
DEVILED GREEN BEANS

WITCHES' BREW

❁ *Halloween*

Customs and superstitions gathered through the ages go into our celebration of Halloween, or All Hallows' Eve, on October 31. The day is so named because it is the eve of the Festival of All Saints, but many of the beliefs and observances connected with it arose long before the Christian era, in the autumn festivals of pagan peoples.

The Druids believed that the spirits of the dead roamed abroad, especially in disguise as cats, ghosts, and witches. They lighted bonfires to drive them away. In ancient Rome, the festival of Pomona, goddess of fruits and gardens, occurred at this time of year. It was an occasion of rejoicing that the harvest was finished, and apples, nuts, corn, and other foods were roasted before huge bonfires.

Even after November 1 became a Christian feast day, the peasants clung to the old pagan beliefs and customs that had grown up about Halloween. It became a night of mystery and fun-making, with many picturesque superstitions, and it also incorporated many of the customs of the harvest festivals.

Today, young and old still gather to hunt nuts, duck for apples, wear costumes and masks, and play tricks. Grinning jack-o'-lanterns, cornstalks, and black paper witches and cats are used for party decorations.

Cauldron Smoke

2 small lemons
1 cup (½ pound) seedless
   raisins, finely chopped

4 quarts boiling water
1 pound sugar

Remove rinds of lemons as thinly as possible and pour boiling water over them. Squeeze juice of lemons and strain. When rinds are cool, add strained lemon juice, raisins, and sugar. Cover and let preparation remain for 5 days, stirring 3 or 4 times daily. Then strain into bottles and refrigerate. This beverage will keep only a short time, about a week. *(Makes approximately fifteen 8-ounce glasses.)*

Applejack Cocktail

1½ ounces applejack
1 teaspoon grenadine

1 teaspoon lemon juice

Shake with cracked ice and strain into cocktail glass.

Cider Cup

1 pint cider
6 ounces club soda
½ ounce Triple Sec or other
   orange-flavored liqueur

½ ounce curaçao
2 ounces brandy
4 teaspoons confectioners' sugar

Fill large pitcher with cubes of ice. Mix all ingredients and pour over ice cubes. Stir well and decorate with as many fruits as available. Serve in 5-ounce wine glasses. *(Makes 6 servings.)*

Sardine Apples

5 ounces cream cheese   ⅛ teaspoon pepper
5 ounces sardines in oil   Paprika
1 tablespoon onion juice   Cloves
1 teaspoon salt

Soften cream cheese and combine with sardines, onion juice, salt, and pepper in a blender. If you haven't got a blender, mash all together until well blended. Roll mixture in small balls. Roll balls in paprika until red all over. Stick whole clove in one side and clove stem in other side for apple stem. Refrigerate until served.

Roquefort Apples

Core unpeeled red apples and slice thinly. Put apple slices in a bowl of half water and half lemon juice to keep them from becoming brown. Mix ½ pound Roquefort or bleu cheese with ¼ cup soft butter and 1 tablespoon brandy. Drain apple slices and spread with cheese mixture. Sprinkle with chopped fresh parsley. Cover and refrigerate until needed.

Broiled Chutney Prunes

Soak large prunes overnight in port wine to cover. Drain prunes, remove pits, and fill cavities with chutney. Wrap each prune in a strip of bacon. Broil until bacon is crisp. Drain on paper and serve hot.

Curried Almonds and Walnuts

¼ cup olive oil   Pinch of cayenne
1 tablespoon curry powder   2 cups shelled walnut halves
1 tablespoon Worcestershire   1 cup blanched almonds
   sauce

Mix all ingredients but nuts in a skillet and heat. When it is very hot, add walnut halves and almonds. Stir nuts until well coated. Spread on paper on a baking sheet and bake in a slow oven (300 degrees) for 10 minutes or until crisp.

Cat Toasts

With a cat-shaped cookie cutter, cut cats from white, pumpernickel, rye, and brown slices of bread. Spread bread cats on a baking sheet, brush with melted butter, and bake in oven until browned. Turn and brown on other side. Pile in a serving dish to be served hot with hors d'oeuvres.

Stuffed Pumpkins

Select 6 small orange pumpkins about 8 inches in diameter and of a uniform size. Slice top from each pumpkin and scoop out seeds and fibers. Sprinkle inside with salt and pepper. Fill each pumpkin with the following mixture. Replace top before baking.

1 cup cooked cubed ham	1 cup chopped green peppers
1 cup cooked diced chicken	1 cup highly seasoned sausage
1 cup chopped onions	1 cup bread crumbs

Saute meat and vegetables together a few minutes until sausage is brown. Mix together and fill pumpkin shells. Top with bread crumbs, dot with butter, and bake in a moderate oven until outside of pumpkin shells can be easily pierced with a fork. Serve whole. *(Makes 6 servings.)*

Hot Pussycats

2 cups flour	1 egg, beaten
½ teaspoon cinnamon	2 tablespoons chopped lemon
¼ teaspoon salt	peel
6 ounces (1½ sticks) butter	4 tablespoons chopped almonds
1 cup brown sugar, firmly	1 tablespoon melted butter
packed	1 egg, separated

Sift flour, cinnamon, and salt. Cream in butter. Add sugar, mix well, add beaten whole egg, and mix to a soft dough. Divide dough in 2 pieces and roll each ⅛-inch thick.

Mix lemon peel, almonds, 1 tablespoon butter, and egg yolk well together. Cut pieces of dough with a cat-shaped cookie cutter. Put lemon-peel mixture between 2 cats and seal edges with tines of a fork dipped in cold water. Brush with egg white and bake at 350 degrees for 30 minutes. Serve hot. *(Makes 6 servings.)*

Lettuce Rosette Salad

6 uniform heads of Bibb or buttercrunch lettuce

STUFFING:

12 block olives, pitted and chopped	2 tablespoons finely chopped onions
6 anchovy filets, chopped	2 tablespoons olive oil
1 tablespoon capers	2 chopped hard-cooked eggs
2 tablespoons chopped parsley	Salt and pepper to taste
1 teaspoon garlic juice	

Spread lettuce leaves and wash carefully without breaking them from stem. Mix stuffing ingredients and spoon between leaves of lettuce, keeping heads of lettuce whole. Pour French dressing over just before serving. *(Makes 6 servings.)*

Deviled Green Beans

4 tablespoons butter	¼ teaspoon salt
1 teaspoon prepared mustard	⅛ teaspoon coarsely ground black pepper
1 teaspoon Worcestershire sauce	
1 teaspoon horseradish	4 cups cooked French-cut green beans
1 teaspoon brown sugar	

Cream butter with rest of ingredients except beans. Toss with hot drained green beans. *(Makes 6 servings.)*

Witches' Brew

1 lemon	1 teaspoon ground cinnamon
1 orange	1 teaspoon ground ginger
3 quarts cider	8 whole cloves
4 tablespoons brown sugar	¾ pint dark rum

Peel fruit very thinly and chop rind. Slice fruit and remove seeds. Put ½-pint cider in a small saucepan with fruit, rind, sugar, and spices. Cover and simmer for 30 minutes.

Pour rest of cider into a large saucepan, and add strained fruit-and-spice liquid. Heat slowly to a comfortable drinking temperature, add rum, and warm but do not boil. (Never overheat any alcohol mixture or all the "power" will evaporate.) Taste, and add more sugar if desired, as the sweetness of cider varies. *(Makes 10 to 12 servings.)*

Thanksgiving Dinner

PLYMOUTH ROCK GOBBLER
HARVEST COCKTAIL
WHISPERS OF THE FROST COCKTAIL

ROAST SPICED TURKEY

ROAST STUFFED SWEET POTATOES
LENTIL SALAD
WITH SOUR CREAM DRESSING

FROZEN PUMPKIN PIE
IN A BRAZIL NUT PIE SHELL

✳ *Thanksgiving*

A quaint old account thus describes the earliest American harvest festival, held in 1621, the exiles' first autumn in their new homeland: "Our harvest being gotten in, our Governour sent foure men on fowling, so that we might after a more special manner rejoyce together after we had gathered the fruit of our labours. They foure in one day killed as much fowle as, with a little help beside, served the company almost a weeke."

Plymouth Rock Gobbler

1 egg	½ teaspoon vinegar
1 teaspoon Worcestershire sauce	1 drop tabasco sauce

Season with a little salt and pepper and serve in a 5-ounce wine glass.

Harvest Cocktail

1½ ounces dry gin	¾ ounce rhubarb syrup

Shake well with cracked ice and strain into cocktail glass.

Whispers of the Frost Cocktail

¾ ounce whiskey
¾ ounce sherry

¾ ounce port wine
1 teaspoon confectioners' sugar

Shake well with cracked ice and strain into a cocktail glass. Serve with slices of lemon and orange.

Roast Spiced Turkey

2 tablespoons flour
1 teaspoon sugar
1 teaspoon salt
1 teaspoon coarsely ground
    black pepper
½ clove garlic, crushed

1 teaspoon ground cinnamon
½ teaspoon ground ginger
10- to 12-pound turkey
2 large onions, chopped
2 tablespoons butter

Mix flour, sugar, salt, pepper, garlic, and spices together with enough warm water to make a paste. Rub the turkey well inside and out with this mixture; cover and let stand at least 12 hours. Put turkey in a large kettle, add onions, and cover with warm water. Bring to a boil slowly, and simmer for 2 hours or until turkey is tender but not falling apart. Drain. Fill with the following stuffing, put in a roasting pan, dot with butter, and bake uncovered in a hot oven until brown, basting occasionally with turkey stock.

STUFFING:

½ pound prunes
1 pound chestnuts
4 pears
1 pound chicken livers
2 tablespoons butter

1 cup white wine
1 teaspoon salt
¼ teaspoon coarsely ground
    black pepper
½ teaspoon nutmeg

Soak, cook, and pit prunes. Shell chestnuts and cook in water until soft. Peel pears and cut into small pieces. (Canned pears may be used.) Chop prunes, livers, and chestnuts, and cook with pears for 10 minutes in butter. Add wine, season with salt, pepper, and grated nutmeg. Stuff turkey with mixture and roast until well browned. *(Makes 6 ample servings.)*

Roast Stuffed Sweet Potatoes

Rub 6 large, uniform sweet potatoes with butter and bake uncovered in a moderate oven, about 350 degrees, until tender. The skin should be crisp and of nut-brown color. Cut hot potatoes in half and scoop out centers. Mash, and whip with the following:

STUFFING:

2 tablespoons bacon fat, melted | 2 teaspoons ground sage
1 tablespoon butter, melted with | 1 teaspoon salt
    bacon fat

Pile lightly into sweet potato shells, sprinkle with grated Parmesan cheese, and brown under broiler. *(Makes 6 servings.)*

Lentil Salad

½ pint lentils | 2 tablespoons chopped parsley
½ pint turkey stock | 2 tablespoons chopped onions

Soak lentils for 2 hours. Cook them gently in stock until tender. Drain and mix with parsley and onions, and serve with Sour Cream Dressing. *(Makes 6 servings.)*

Sour Cream Dressing

1 egg yolk, beaten | 1 tablespoon chopped parsley
2 tablespoons tarragon vinegar | ¼ teaspoon coarsely ground
½ pint sour cream | black pepper
1 tablespoon chopped onions | 1 teaspoon chopped tarragon

Mix egg yolk with vinegar and blend in rest of ingredients. *(Makes about 1½ cups.)*

Frozen Pumpkin Pie

1 cup confectioners' sugar | 1½ cups mashed cooked (or
1 teaspoon cinnamon | canned) pumpkin
1 teaspoon powdered ginger | ⅔ cup heavy cream, whipped
½ teaspoon salt | 9-inch Brazil Nut Pie Shell
3 eggs, separated

Add sugar, spices, salt, and slightly beaten egg yolks to pumpkin and cook over boiling water until thickened. Fold in stiffly beaten egg whites, then whipped cream. Pour into refrigerator tray and partially freeze. Pack into Brazil Nut Pie Shell and keep frozen until ready to use.

Brazil Nut Pie Shell

1⅔ cups ground Brazil nuts | 4 tablespoons sugar

Mix nuts with sugar. Line pie pan with mixture by pressing it firmly into place. *(Makes one 9-inch pie shell.)*

Yankee Christmas Eve
Tree=Trimming Party

AMERICAN GROG
ROYAL EGGNOG

OYSTER HASH

HOMINY A LA OLD HOUSE

CRANBERRY SALAD
WITH CRANBERRY MAYONNAISE

MINCEMEAT MACAROONS

American Grog

1½ ounces Jamaica rum
1 teaspoon blackstrap molasses
  or sorghum

1 tablespoon lemon juice
Hot water or hot tea

Stir in a large mug, adding hot water or hot tea last. Sprinkle with grated lemon rind.

Royal Eggnog

2 quarts vanilla ice cream
4 cups hot strong coffee

4 cups whiskey
1 cup light rum

Mix ice cream and coffee until ice cream melts. Stir in whiskey and rum. Sprinkle with grated nutmeg. *(Makes 4 quarts.)*

Oyster Hash

1 pint raw oysters
1 cup coarsely chopped onions
1 cup coarsely chopped celery
½ cup chopped green pepper
2 tablespoons butter or
   margarine
1 cup raw potato cubes
1 teaspoon salt
¼ teaspoon coarsely ground
   black pepper
½ teaspoon thyme
½ cup sauterne

Cook oysters in own liquid for just 5 minutes, until they are plumped and their edges curled. Set aside. In a skillet, saute onions, celery, and green pepper in butter or margarine until onions are soft but not colored. Use a low heat, keep skillet covered, and stir frequently. Add potato cubes and liquor drained from cooked oysters. Add salt, pepper, and thyme. Cover and cook over low heat until potatoes are done. Stir from time to time and keep skillet covered. Add oysters and sauterne and cook 5 minutes more, or until oysters are heated through. Spoon hash into chafing dish with a hot-water underpan and keep hot on buffet. *(Makes 6 servings.)*

Hominy à la Old House

2 cups cooked large hominy
1 cup grated Swiss cheese
3 eggs, slightly beaten
1 teaspoon salt
1 teaspoon Worcestershire sauce
1 tablespoon chopped chives
1 tablespoon chopped parsley
1 tablespoon chopped
   pimientoes
1¼ cups light cream, scalded

Heat oven to 350 degrees. Combine all ingredients and pour into a well-buttered casserole. Bake uncovered at 350 degrees in a pan of hot water for 30 minutes, or until set. *(Makes 6 servings.)*

Cranberry Salad

2 cups fresh cranberries
1½ cups cold water
1 cup sugar
1 tablespoon unflavored gelatin
½ cup chopped nuts
¾ cup diced celery
¾ cup diced unpeeled red
   apples
½ cup minced onion

Wash cranberries, and add 1 cup cold water. Cook until tender or popping. Add sugar and cook 5 minutes longer. Soften gelatin in ½ cup cold water, then dissolve in hot cranberries. Chill until mixture thickens slightly. Add rest of ingredients and pour into an oiled mold. Chill until firm. Unmold and serve on salad greens with Cranberry Mayonnaise. *(Makes 6 servings.)*

Cranberry Mayonnaise

2 teaspoons salt	½ cup honey
1 teaspoon dry mustard	2 cups salad oil
½ teaspoon black pepper	¼ cup tarragon vinegar
½ teaspoon ground ginger	2 cups minced fresh cranberries
2 egg yolks	

Combine dry ingredients with unbeaten egg yolks in a mixing bowl and beat together until stiff. Add honey and beat thoroughly. Add part of oil, beating it into mixture drop by drop at first, then pouring more rapidly, always keeping mixture stiff. When it begins to thicken, add a little vinegar. Alternate rest of oil and vinegar until well blended. Stir in cranberries.

Mincemeat Macaroons

1½ cups flour	½ cup sugar
¼ teaspoon salt	1 egg, well beaten
½ teaspoon baking soda	¾ cup moist mincemeat
5 tablespoons butter	¼ teaspoon vanilla

Sift flour, salt, and soda together. Cream butter, add sugar, and blend well. Add egg to butter and sugar. Combine with dry ingredients. Fold in mincemeat. Add vanilla and mix. Drop by teaspoonfuls 2 or 3 inches apart on a greased baking sheet. Bake at 375 degrees 10 to 15 minutes. *(Makes 2 dozen macaroons.)*

English Christmas Dinner

BEER FLIP
OLD HOUSE WASSAIL BOWL
WELSH CRANBERRY NECTAR

BOAR'S HEAD CENTERPIECE
ROAST GOOSE
ROAST BARON OF BEEF
ONIONS BAKED IN GOOSE CRACKLINGS
VICTORIA'S CUCUMBER MANDRAM
CARROT PUFFS
JUGGED CELERY

ROYAL CHRISTMAS PUDDING
DUBLIN ROCK

Beer Flip

1 quart strong beer or ale	¼ teaspoon ground cloves
8 egg yolks, beaten	¼ teaspoon ground nutmeg
½ cup sugar	¼ teaspoon ground cinnamon
1 cup orange juice	8 egg whites, beaten stiff

Heat beer or ale very hot but not boiling. Pour in egg yolks, sugar, juice, and spices, then pour back into pan again from a height, so that it froths high. Add stiffly beaten egg whites to the froth and serve swiftly while hot. *(Makes about 10 punch cups.)*

Old House Wassail Bowl

1 pound brown sugar	1 whole grated nutmeg
1 pint beer, heated very hot but not boiling	2 cups dry sherry
	5 pints cold beer
2 tablespoons preserved ginger, chopped	Yeast
	6 slices toasted brown bread

Mix sugar, hot beer, spices, and sherry, and stir well. When cooled, dilute with cold beer. Spread a suspicion of yeast on toasted brown bread. Add to cold liquid. Let stand, covered, for 6 hours. Strain, bottle, and seal. In a few days it should be popping the corks. Then strain into a large decorative bowl and serve hot with roasted apples floated in it. *(Makes about 30 punch cups.)*

Welsh Cranberry Nectar

2 tablespoons whole cloves
1 tablespoon whole allspice
12 inches stick cinnamon,
 broken in pieces
¼ cup brown sugar
4 cups water
¼ teaspoon salt
4 cups unsweetened pineapple
 juice

4 cups (two 1-pound cans)
 jellied cranberry sauce
Few drops red food coloring
1 fifth vodka
Butter
Orange slices
Cinnamon sticks

Tie whole cloves and allspice in small piece of cheesecloth. In a saucepan place the spice bag, cinnamon pieces, brown sugar, 1 cup water, and salt. Bring slowly to a boil. Add pineapple juice and 3 cups water. Crush cranberry sauce with a fork and add. Bring to a boil again and simmer for 5 minutes. Remove spices. Add a few drops of red food coloring. Pour into a heated bowl and stir in vodka. Add a few dots of butter on top. Float clove-studded thin orange slices, cut in half. Serve in mugs with cinnamon sticks as stirrers. *(Makes about 12 cups.)*

Boar's Head Centerpiece

This is an ambitious project, but a real showpiece. You will have to order your boar's head in advance from your butcher, and ask him to prepare it for roasting. It should be split in half except for the joining skin at the top. Eyes and all bone at the back should be removed. Place the head down flat and soak it in cold water for an hour, changing the water two or three times while it is soaking. Leave overnight completely covered with strong salt water.

Next day, drain boar's head, wipe dry, and rub it well with salt and saltpeter, in the proportion of 1 dram of saltpeter to 2 tablespoons salt mixed with pickling spice and coarsely ground black pepper. (Saltpeter is available by the dram at drugstores.) Put a 3-inch wooden block between the jaws to wedge the mouth open while cooking. Wrap ears in wet cloths and then wrap the cloths in foil. Skewer the head back into shape, and wrap it completely in foil. Roast at 350 degrees, allowing 1 hour for each pound of weight. Remove all foil and ear protectors, and return to oven at 325 degrees until well browned all over. Remove boar's head and cool overnight.

Place a polished red apple in the boar's mouth. Make a stiff glaze as follows:

2 envelopes unflavored plain gelatin	**2 cups boiling water**
1 cup cold water	**½ cup vinegar**

Sprinkle gelatin on cold water to soften. Add boiling water and vinegar. Stir until thoroughly dissolved. Chill slightly until gelatin just begins to set.

Have ready a collection of pimientos, green peppers, hard-cooked egg slices, olives, etc., to cut into decorative tiny circles, diamonds, squares. One of the prettiest color combinations is sliced stuffed olives, circles from ripe black olives, lemon peel, orange peel, and red radishes.

It is best to work in a cold place so that the gelatin sets immediately upon being spread on the boar's head. If the weather is cold, you might do your decorating outdoors. Be sure that the boar's head is quite cold when you start — that will also make the gelatin set up fast. First spoon a good coating of gelatin over the entire head. On the boar's forehead, make a poinsettia with petals cut from whole canned red pimentos, and green pepper strips for the stems and leaves. Arrange the rest of the decorations according to your taste and imagination. If you have trouble getting the decorations to stay in place, use pins. Pin a collar of holly leaves and fresh red cranberries around the neck.

After placing the decorations where you want them, spoon the gelatin over them evenly. If your gelatin gets too thick, simply reheat it a little to melt it to the right consistency for pouring or spreading. Keep the finished boar's head cold until you are ready to use it, but do not let it freeze or the gelatin will split and break.

After using the boar's head for a centerpiece, you can if you wish carve the meat on it lengthwise and eat as a savory cold spiced bacon. Or you can fry the slices and get a hot, crisp spiced bacon.

Roast Goose

10-pound goose	Powdered coriander
Salt and pepper	2 cups hot water
Sweet basil	

STUFFING:

12 large oysters	4 apples, peeled, cored, and
½ cup oyster liquor	sliced
1 tablespoon butter	4 large onions, sliced
1 tablespoon dried parsley flakes	2 teaspoons ground sage
1 teaspoon grated lemon rind	1 teaspoon lemon thyme
½ teaspoon salt	2 cups mashed potatoes
¼ teaspoon pepper	

Wipe goose inside and out. Sprinkle inside with salt, pepper, and sweet basil.

To make stuffing: Simmer first 7 ingredients together 5 minutes and remove from heat. Boil apples, onions, sage, and thyme with just enough water to cover them. When done, rub them through a sieve. Add to oysters. Add enough mashed mealy potatoes so that stuffing will be dry and won't stick to your hand. Season with salt and pepper to taste, and stuff bird. Truss legs for roasting.

Prick goose all over with a fork and place on a rack in a roasting pan. Sprinkle goose with coriander. Put hot water in bottom of pan, cover pan, and roast goose about 2 hours, or until tender. Remove cover and brown. *(Makes 6 to 8 servings.)*

Pour goose grease and stock from bottom of roaster into a covered jar and store in the refrigerator. There is no seasoning in the world as good as this, for either meats or vegetables.

Baron of Beef, the Roast Beef of Old England

For this you need an entire sirloin cut, about 10 to 15 pounds. Place sirloin in roasting pan and cover with the following marinade:

1 cup salad oil	1 tablespoon dried parsley flakes
1 onion, cut into thin slices	2 tablespoons lemon juice
1 clove garlic, mashed	1 tablespoon coarsely ground
1 teaspoon thyme	black pepper
1 bay leaf, crushed	

144

Turn roast over from time to time in this marinade and let meat absorb flavors and oil for several hours. Before roasting, remove onion slices. Fold sirloin with fat part on top. Sprinkle generously with salt and coarse black pepper. It will baste itself. Roast in a preheated oven at 450 degrees for 20 minutes, then continue at 350 degrees, allowing 10 minutes per pound for rare and 15 minutes for medium or pink inside. Slice against the grain to serve. It is good either hot or cold. *(Rare, makes 20 to 30 servings; medium or well-done, makes 15 to 25 servings.)*

Yorkshire Pudding

2 cups sifted flour
1 teaspoon salt
2 cups milk
1 cup cream

4 eggs
8 tablespoons beef drippings
   from roast

Sift flour and salt into a mixing bowl. Slowly stir in milk and cream, beating until smooth. Add eggs, one at a time, beating constantly to make a creamy batter. Cover with a cloth and chill in refrigerator for 2 hours.

Thirty minutes before roast is done, spoon drippings from roast into a shallow baking pan and set it in oven until sizzling hot. Beat chilled batter a few minutes and pour it into hot drippings about ½-inch deep. Bake in a very hot oven for 15 minutes. After pudding rises, lower heat to 325 degrees and bake for 15 minutes longer, or until pudding is light, crisp, and brown. Cut pudding in squares and serve with roast.

Onions Baked in Goose Cracklings

Peel large Bermuda onions and place tightly side by side in a casserole. Chop skin of the Christmas goose and mix with a sufficient amount of goose grease and drippings from roast goose to fill spaces between onions. Bake in a 350-degree oven, covered, for 1 hour. Remove cover and brown onions lightly before serving.

Victoria's Cucumber Mandram

Cut a peeled cucumber in large cubes. Add an equal quantity of spring onions cut into small rounds and an equal quantity of cold cooked pearl barley. Shake together and season with the juice of a lemon, white pepper, and a pinch of salt. Chill and serve in crisp lettuce cups.

Carrot Puffs
An eighteenth-century recipe still very popular in England's finest inns

Scrape, boil, and mash very fine enough carrots to make 2 cups. Mix with 1 cup brown bread crumbs. Separate yolks and whites of 6 eggs. Beat whites until stiff and in peaks. Stir yolks in with carrots and crumbs, mixing well. Stir in 2 tablespoons orange-flower water, ¼ teaspoon grated nutmeg, ¼ teaspoon salt, and 1 tablespoon sugar. Add 1 cup heavy cream and mix well. Fold in beaten egg whites. Drop by spoonfuls into very hot cooking oil. Cook puffs until browned, and drain on paper. These will be very light. *(Makes 6 servings.)*

Jugged Celery
An old Cornish dish

For this you will need a deep-sided stewpan, casserole, or widemouthed jug. Cover bottom of jug with slices of bacon. Rub sides with bacon fat or drippings. To 1 cup applesauce, add ¼ teaspoon ground cloves and 1 teaspoon salt, and pour applesauce into jug. Pack into the jug, in an upright position, as many stalks of celery as you can wedge in, until pot is full. By that time the applesauce will have risen to the top. Trim celery stalks off level, and cover top ends with finely chopped bacon. Cover and bake at 350 degrees for 1 hour, or until celery is tender.

Royal Christmas Pudding

1½ pounds suet	½ cup citron peel
2½ cups demerara sugar (a light brown, large-crystal sugar, very sweet) or raw sugar (carried in most gourmet shops; Old House Epicurean stocks it)	½ cup candied orange peel
	1 teaspoon mace
	½ teaspoon nutmeg
	6 cups bread crumbs
	2 cups sifted flour
	8 grade A large eggs
3 cups raisins	1 cup milk
3 cups sultanas	½ cup brandy

Mix all dry ingredients. Beat eggs well, add to milk, and mix well. Mix dry ingredients and eggs. Let stand 12 hours in cool place; add brandy and put into a well-greased pan. Bake in a slow oven at 250 degrees for 8 hours. *(Makes 20 to 25 servings.)*

146

Dublin Rock
An 1890 sweet, a form of marchpane of earlier times, or marzipan of today

4 ounces (1 stick) sweet butter	3 tablespoons confectioners'
½ pound almonds, ground	sugar
1½ tablespoons brandy	3 drops orange-flower water

Heat an earthenware bowl really hot and melt butter in it. Beat almonds, sugar, and brandy into butter or cream. Add orange-flower water and continue to beat until bowl is cold and mixture sets light, white, and stiff. Leave it until it sets stiff. Next day break it into rough lumps — it should be soft but firm. Pile the chunks up on a platter like craggy rocks. Sprinkle with angelica and split almonds.

New Year's Eve Buffet

NEW YEAR'S EVE PUNCH

MIXED GREEN SALAD
WITH SPICY DRESSING

STEAK AND MUSHROOM CASSEROLE
POTATO ROLLS

HOLIDAY CREAM TARTS

New Year's Eve Punch

½ cup cognac
½ cup orange curaçao
½ cup maraschino liqueur
3 lemons, thinly sliced
4 oranges, thinly sliced

1 pint raspberries (fresh,
  canned, or frozen)
6 bottles champagne, well
  chilled

Mix all ingredients except champagne in a large punch bowl and chill for at least an hour before using. At serving time, add champagne. Do not add any ice to the punch. It will have plenty of punch! *(Makes 30 cups.)*

Mixed Green Salad

1 cup torn chicory leaves
1 large head lettuce, torn up
1 cup fresh crisp spinach leaves,
  torn up
1 cup fresh celery tops, coarsely
  chopped

1 cup romaine, cut up
1 cup chopped leeks (tops and
  bottoms)
1 cup raw paper-thin slices
  kohlrabi

Combine greens, leeks, and kohlrabi in a large salad bowl and toss with Spicy Dressing. *(Makes 24 servings.)*

Spicy Dressing

¾ cup tarragon vinegar
1¾ cups salad oil
¼ cup grated onion
3 bay leaves, crumbled

1 teaspoon chili powder
½ teaspoon cayenne pepper
1 teaspoon salt

Combine all ingredients in a jar. Shake well before using. *(Makes about 3 cups.)*

Steak and Mushroom Casserole

24 beef tenderloin steaks (about 6 ounces each)
1 pound (4 sticks) butter
6 pounds fresh mushroom caps without stems (6 dozen 2-inch caps)
6 large Bermuda or white onions, sliced
6 cans condensed cream of mushroom soup

3 cups thick sour cream
12 tablespoons chopped or minced parsley
3 tablespoons salt
1½ teaspoons coarsely ground black pepper
1½ teaspoons dry mustard
6 cans (4 ounces each) julienne-style sliced pimientos
1 tablespoon thyme

Flatten steaks slightly and saute in butter until browned. Remove to platter. Wash mushroom caps and shake off excess water but do not dry. To pan juices add mushroom caps and sliced onions. Cover pan and cook until onions are soft but not browned and liquid has been reduced to not quite dry, approximately 15 minutes. Add rest of ingredients and mix well. Correct seasoning to taste. Combine sauteed steaks with mushrooms and sauce, mix well, and put into well-buttered baking pans. This dish may be made ahead and kept in the refrigerator or freezer until needed. Bake 1 hour at 350 degrees just before serving. *(Makes 24 servings.)*

Potato Rolls

1 cake yeast
½ cup lukewarm water
5 tablespoons sugar
½ cup (1 stick) butter, plus a little extra, melted
1 cup milk

1 cup hot mashed potatoes
1 egg, beaten
1 teaspoon salt
6 cups sifted flour
Chopped dried chervil

Crumble yeast into bowl and add warm water and 1 tablespoon sugar. Let stand 5 minutes. Cream ½ cup butter and remaining sugar. Add milk to mashed potatoes and combine with butter mixture. Cool to lukewarm.

Add potatoes to yeast mixture with egg and salt. Beat in 2 cups flour. Let rise until light. Knead in remaining flour and continue kneading until dough is satiny. Place in lightly greased bowl. Grease top of dough. Cover, put into refrigerator, and let chill for 12 hours.

Take dough out of refrigerator and punch down. Let stand at room temperature for 1 hour. Shape into rolls. Put rolls in greased pans, cover, and let rise until doubled in bulk.

Brush rolls with melted butter and sprinkle tops with chopped dried chervil. Bake at 425 degrees for 20 minutes. *(Makes about 30 rolls.)*

Holiday Cream Tarts

1 cup dark seedless raisins	1 quart plus ½ cup milk
1 cup golden seedless raisins	9 egg yolks (¾ cup), beaten
1 cup candied fruit and peels mixed	⅓ cup light molasses
	1 tablespoon vanilla
3 tablespoons unflavored gelatin	1½ tablespoons brandy
¾ cup cold water	9 egg whites (1⅛ cups)
¾ cup sifted flour	¾ teaspoon cream of tartar
3 cups sugar	1½ cups heavy whipping cream
1½ teaspoons salt	2 dozen 3-inch baked tart shells
¾ teaspoon nutmeg	

Chop raisins and candied fruits coarsely. Soften gelatin in cold water. Sift together flour, 2 cups sugar, salt, and nutmeg. Combine with milk. Cook and stir until mixture thickens. Remove from heat. Carefully stir in egg yolks. Add softened gelatin, molasses, and vanilla and brandy. Cool. Chill until mixture thickens to mound on a spoon. Add raisins and candied fruits. Beat egg whites with cream of tartar until foamy. Gradually add remaining sugar, beating until stiff peaks form. Whip cream. Fold meringue into gelatin mixture. Fold in whipped cream. Spoon into baked and thoroughly cooled tart shells. Chill until firm. *(Makes 24 cream tarts.)*

"Home Is the Hunter"
Dinner

RUSSIAN BEAR COCKTAIL

SALTY DOG

ELK'S OWN COCKTAIL

HUNTSMAN COCKTAIL

VENISON

ROAST—STEAKS—STEW—SADDLE—CHOPS

WILD GOOSE

STEW—ROAST—CRACKLINGS

ROAST WOODCOCKS, GROUSE, SNIPES, PLOVERS

SAN QUENTIN QUAIL

WILD DUCK

BLACKBIRD PIE

BRAISED RABBIT OR HARE

PHEASANT A LA OLD HOUSE

BACKWOODS PIE

Russian Bear Cocktail

1 ounce vodka   ½ ounce crème de cacao
½ ounce sweet cream

Stir well with cracked ice and strain into 3-ounce cocktail glass.

Salty Dog

Fill 12-ounce glass almost full with shaved ice or ice cubes and add 2 ounces dry gin, 4 ounces grapefruit juice, and a pinch of salt. Stir well.

Elk's Own Cocktail

1 egg white
1½ ounces rye or bourbon
   whiskey

¾ ounces port wine
Juice of ¼ lemon
1 teaspoon confectioners' sugar

Shake well with cracked ice, strain into 4-ounce cocktail glass, and add a strip of pineapple.

Huntsman Cocktail

1½ ounces vodka
½ ounce Jamaica rum

Juice of ½ lime
Confectioners' sugar to taste

Shake well with cracked ice and strain into 3-ounce cocktail glass.

Venison

Buck venison is best from August to November, doe venison from November to January. The female deer furnishes the best venison at the age of about four years.

It is a common custom to freeze venison and keep it for months. Without doubt, freezing improves the fiber of the meat, which is a little on the tough side, depending upon the age of the animal. The fatter venison is, the better. If the animal was young, the meat will be completely lean and a dark red.

The main cuts of venison are as follows:
- Shoulder: used for roasts. It can be boned and stuffed.
- Foreloin: furnishes steaks and roasts.
- Saddle (middle of back): makes a fine roast.
- Haunch (whole hind quarter): used for steaks, roasts, stews, pickled and smoked cuts.
- Breast: used for baked dishes and stews.
- Neck: goes into soups only.

Marinade for Venison

Regardless of the cut or age of venison, it should be marinated to help tenderize it before cooking. This is a good marinade for all cuts:

1 medium-size carrot, sliced very thin	1 tablespoon salt
6 tablespoons chopped onions	1 teaspoon black pepper
2 tablespoons diced celery	1 teaspoon ground cloves
1 clove garlic, mashed	6 coriander seeds, crushed
1 teaspoon chopped parsley	6 juniper berries, crushed
¼ teaspoon thyme	3 cups dry white wine
1 bay leaf, crushed	1½ cups salad oil

Mix all ingredients. Put meat in a deep container just large enough to hold it. Pour marinade over meat and turn it often so that the flavors will impregnate it completely. (An even better marinade can be made by substituting papaya juice for the wine. Bottled papaya concentrate is available at good gourmet shops.)

Roast Haunch of Venison

This is the choicest piece for roasting. Let it stand in the above marinade for at least 24 hours. Roast in a 450-degree oven until the meat is tender, basting every 15 minutes with the marinade and melted butter. When meat is tender, strain gravy or juice and add 2 tablespoons currant jelly to it. To serve, slice meat against the grain, and pour sauce over it.

Venison Steaks

Cut steaks ¾-inch thick. Marinate in the above for at least 24 hours, turning occasionally. Remove steaks and drain.

In a skillet put 3 tablespoons olive oil and saute steaks over a high heat 3 minutes on each side. Remove steaks and keep hot. Drain excess fat from skillet, and to the juices remaining add 2 tablespoons butter and 2 chopped green onions. Cook until onions are soft. Stir in 1 tablespoon flour, and stir and cook until flour is browned. Add 4 tablespoons wine and 1 cup thick sour cream.

Cook, stirring constantly, until sauce is thickened and smooth. Correct seasoning to taste and pour over steaks to serve.

Venison Stew

Cut venison into 2-inch cubes. Marinate in the above 2 hours. To every 4 cups of meat cubes, add 1½ cups dry red wine, 1 cup water, and 4 tablespoons marinade. Simmer over medium heat for about 2 hours or until meat is tender, adding wine and water if needed. When meat is done, add carrots, potatoes, onions, and turnips, and cook until vegetables are done.

Roast Saddle of Venison

Remove second skin from the saddle and trim off all sinews. Cover saddle with the above marinade and let stand for 2 days, turning frequently so that marinade will penetrate meat evenly. Remove meat from marinade and drain.

Place meat in a roasting pan with strips of bacon laid across top. Sprinkle with salt and pepper. Roast meat in a hot oven at 450 degrees, basting frequently with butter. If you like rare venison, allow 10 minutes per pound.

Venison Cutlets or Chops

Put cutlets or chops in a deep vessel and cover with the above marinade, turning frequently, for 2 hours. Remove meat, drain, and panbroil over high heat. Serve with Jelly Sauce.

Jelly Sauce

Strain the above marinade into a pan to make 1 pint juices. Thicken with 1 tablespoon browned flour; add 2 tablespoons currant jelly, 1 tablespoon lemon juice, and salt and pepper to taste. Pour over cutlets or chops.

Wild Goose

Geese live to a great age, but they are not tender if over 3 years old. A young goose has down on its legs, and the legs are soft and yellow, like a young turkey's. And, like a turkey, as a goose grows older its legs change to a reddish color. Therefore, if you bag a tough old bird, it is best to make it into a stew.

Goose Stew (Wild or domestic)

Clean and dress goose for cooking. Wrap goose in foil or freezer paper and freeze it overnight (freezing will help to tenderize it). When goose is partially thawed but still cold, use a sharp knife to cut skin down the backbone, around base of neck and wings, and around first joint of the legs. Then use a dull knife to lift the skin and layer of fat in large pieces off the flesh underneath. In some places, the skin and fat will come off easily, and in others you must be careful not to cut into the flesh.

As you cut off pieces of fat and skin, drop them into a kettle of cold water or ice water. Keep for Goose Cracklings.

Cut the goose into serving pieces. Put the pieces into a deep pot, and cover with water. In olden times, it was the custom to wash a little lump of coal the size of a walnut and drop it in with the bird. Nobody knows what benefit this had, but if you have a lump of coal, there's no harm in trying it!

Simmer, covered, for an hour, or until the bird is tender. From time to time, skim off fat that rises to top. Put the skimmed fat in the refrigerator to be used later. When the bird is tender, remove the coal, and add:

1 cup sliced carrots	1 cup diced potatoes
1 cup sliced turnips	2 whole cloves
1 cup sliced onions	½ teaspoon thyme
1 cup shredded cabbage	Salt and pepper to taste

Cook slowly, with just enough broth to cover meat and vegetables. When vegetables are done, serve stew in a tureen with tiny biscuits on top. *(Makes 6 servings.)*

Roast Young Wild Goose

1 young wild goose, cleaned

STUFFING:

1 quart toasted bread crumbs	6 apples, peeled, cored, and
2 onions, chopped	sliced thickly
1 teaspoon sage	¼ cup brown sugar
2 teaspoons salt	3 cooked mashed sweet potatoes
¼ teaspoon coarsely ground	Gizzard, heart, and liver cooked
black pepper	until tender in a little butter,
½ teaspoon cardamom seeds,	and chopped
crushed	

Stuff goose and place on a rack in a roasting pan. Put 1 cup water in bottom of pan to steam bird while roasting. Prick bird all over with a two-tined fork to permit fat to ooze out into pan. Roast covered, allowing 20 minutes per pound, until goose is tender. Uncover goose and roast until browned. *(Makes 6 servings.)*

Pour hot drippings in bottom of pan into a glass jar and refrigerate. There is no better seasoning for vegetables in all the world.

Goose Cracklings

Goose grease has always been highly prized for flavoring. The heavy feeding of geese to produce large livers for pâté de foie gras also produces a large amount of clear yellow fat just under the skin. Wild geese have much less of this fatty deposit than domestic geese.

After removing the fat and skin, cut it into 1½-inch squares, sprinkle with salt, and let stand 12 hours. Wash well and drain. Add just enough cold water to cover, and simmer for 1 hour. Water is added to prevent fat from browning too rapidly, and also to permit the steam to carry away any strong flavor the fat might have, leaving the cracklings with a delicate flavor.

Drain and fry slowly to prevent scorching. Fry cracklings until well browned, and then place them in the oven a few minutes. Drain on paper. These are delicious as appetizers. Also delicious when added to corn bread or biscuits.

Roast Woodcocks, Grouse, Snipes, or Plovers

Dress birds, cutting off feet, legs, and necks, and wings at the second joint from tip.

In a baking dish, place a thick slice of toast under each bird. Sprinkle birds inside and out with salt and pepper. Lay a thin slice of orange on each breast, and cover orange slice with thin strips of bacon. Roast at 400 degrees uncovered, basting with a little melted butter, for 35 minutes, or until birds are done. Serve with the toast under each bird.

San Quentin Quail

Dress 6 quail, removing heads, feet, and wing tips. Stuff each quail with white grapes, a bit of chopped onion, and chopped parsley, and sprinkle with freshly ground black pepper and salt. Put quail into a bowl, pour 1 cup of brandy over them, and marinate for 1 hour. Drain off marinade and bring it to a boil with ¼ teaspoon thyme, ½ bay leaf, ½ cup diced celery. Simmer sauce for 1 hour.

Cover breasts of quail with strips of bacon. In a roasting pan, melt 6 tablespoons butter. Arrange quail in butter and roast them in a hot oven (450 degrees) for 15 or 20 minutes. Remove bacon strips and allow quail to brown.

Place each bird on a round of bread that has been fried in butter, and put some white grapes around birds. Heat birds and grapes together in a moderate oven.

To juices in pan, add ½ cup muscatel, bring to a boil, and cook over high heat until reduced by half. Add boiled marinade and bring to a boil again. Mix 1 teaspoon flour to a paste with 1 tablespoon butter, stir into sauce, and cook, stirring, until sauce is slightly thickened. Season to taste and add 1 teaspoon lemon juice. Pour sauce over quail, grapes, and toast rounds, and serve immediately. *(Makes 6 servings.)*

Wild Duck

Ducks shot in the fall after a summer in their northern feeding grounds have a fine flavor. In dressing wild ducks, pluck the large feathers dry. An easy way to remove the down is to melt ½-pound paraffin in 6 quarts boiling water. Dip duck in this mixture several times, until entire body is coated well. Let paraffin cool on duck, then strip off paraffin and down at the same time. Singe what little down is left.

Nearly all wild ducks are likely to have a fishy flavor. Before cooking in any manner, parboil for 15 minutes with a small peeled carrot. Remove duck and drain. Rub duck with butter, and sprinkle inside and out with salt, pepper, and nutmeg. Stuff with the following:

STUFFING FOR TWO 2½-POUND DUCKS:

4 cups soft bread crumbs	2 eggs, beaten
1 cup diced celery	1 cup diced mustard pickle
1 cup diced onion	¼ cup Worcestershire sauce
1 cup seedless raisins	¼ cup A-1 sauce
1 cup chopped nuts	½ cup chili sauce
½ teaspoon salt	6 slices bacon
2 tablespoons brown sugar	1 tablespoon tart plum jelly
½ cup milk, scalded	1 tablespoon kirsch

Mix all dry ingredients, then add all liquid ingredients except plum jelly and kirsch. Place bacon slices on breasts of ducks, and wrap each duck in foil. Place in a roaster and roast at 350 degrees, allowing 15 minutes per pound.

Unwrap foil and roast 10 minutes longer, or until ducks are well browned and bacon is crisp. Pour drippings in foil wrappers into a saucepan and stir in jelly and kirsch. Bring to a boil, and pour over ducks to serve. *(Makes 4 servings.)*

Blackbird Pie
Pigeons, quails, or doves may be substituted

You will need 12 blackbirds, cleaned and dressed. Cut them in halves, put into a baking pan, baste with melted butter, sprinkle with salt and pepper, and bake in a hot oven for 45 minutes, basting with the melted butter every 10 minutes. Remove from oven. Set pan aside. Line a 2-quart deep pan or a raised pie mold with plain pastry.

Have ready 1 pound ham, diced, and 6 hard-cooked eggs, sliced. Put a layer of blackbirds in the bottom, then ham, then eggs, then salt, pepper, and a few bits of butter, then another layer of birds, and so on, until all are used. Cover with a thick sheet of pastry. Make a hole in the center, and ornament the pie with some leaves and flowers cut out of pastry trimmings. Bake in a hot oven (450 degrees) for 30 minutes, or until pastry is done.

Put 2 tablespoons butter in pan in which birds were first baked. Stir over heat until butter and drippings are a nice brown, then add 2 tablespoons flour and mix until smooth. Add 1 pint boiling water, salt and pepper to taste. Stir constantly until sauce boils. Take from heat and add beaten yolk of 1 egg. Stir in 1 tablespoon dry sherry and mix well. Pour into pie through a funnel placed in hole in top crust, and pie is ready to serve. It is delicious. *(Makes 6 servings.)*

Rabbit or Hare

Young wild rabbits will have soft paws and ears. If old, the ears will be stiff, with rough edges, and the paws hard and worn. Young rabbits may be stuffed and roasted whole, but old rabbits are best braised.

Braised Rabbit

Cut a dressed rabbit into serving pieces and dust with flour, salt, and pepper. In a large skillet brown rabbit pieces in 1/4 pound butter, but do not let butter burn. When pieces are browned on all sides, lower heat, add 2/3 cup dry white wine, and simmer, covered, for 1 hour, or until rabbit is tender. Soak 1 teaspoon dried tarragon leaves in 1/4 cup white wine for 30 minutes. Pour over rabbit, and cook for another 5 minutes, turning pieces to cover all with the tarragon. Remove rabbit and keep hot. To pan juices, add 1 teaspoon Kitchen Bouquet, stir, and pour over rabbit. *(Makes 2 to 3 servings.)*

Pheasant à la Old House

Clean and dress 3 plump pheasants. Cut pheasants in half and sprinkle them on both sides with salt and pepper. Saute pheasants in butter until browned. Peel and core 8 tart green apples and slice thickly. Cook apples in a little butter for a few minutes and put in bottom of a well-buttered large casserole or baking pan.

On top of apples put a layer of sliced mushrooms. Put browned birds on top of apples and mushrooms, and pour butter in which birds were browned over the breasts. Cover casserole and bake birds slowly for about 1 hour. Add ½ cup cream, ½ cup apple brandy, 1 teaspoon salt, and ¼ teaspoon coarsely ground black pepper. Cover casserole, and return to oven until sauce is thick and birds are tender. *(Makes 6 servings.)*

Backwoods Pie

4 tablespoons brown sugar
¾ cup maple syrup
½ cup milk
2 tablespoons butter

1 teaspoon nutmeg
3 eggs, separated
1 short crust (rich, flaky) pastry

Beat all pie-filling ingredients together except egg whites. Beat egg whites stiff and fold them into mixture. Line a pie pan with short crust. Pour mixture in. Bake in a preheated 400-degree oven 5 minutes, then turn heat to 350 degrees and bake for 30 to 40 minutes.

Hunt Brunch

THE HUNTER'S CUP
HOT SPICED CIDER
STRAWBERRIES AND CREAM

ESCALOPE OF HAM AND EGGS
SWEET POTATO PONE
EGGPLANT PICKLE

HONEY NUT COFFEE CAKE

The Hunter's Cup

Use a samovar or a large coffee server and keep it hot over a flame.

1 gallon (16 cups) strong black
  coffee
1 pint Jamaica rum

1 quart-size bowl whipped
  cream, beaten stiff with sugar

Mix coffee with rum and keep hot. Place bowl of whipped cream beside it. Allow guests to pour their own cups and spoon blobs of whipped cream on top. *(Makes 24 average-size coffee cups.)*

Hot Spiced Cider

½ cup brown sugar
¼ teaspoon salt
2 quarts cider
1 teaspoon whole allspice

1 teaspoon whole cloves
3-inch stick cinnamon
Orange slices

Combine brown sugar, salt, and cider. Add spices. Slowly bring to a boil and simmer covered for 20 minutes. Strain and serve hot. Float clove-studded orange slices on top. Serve in mugs. *(Makes 10 servings.)*

Strawberries and Cream

Fill a cold deep punch bowl half full of whipped cream that is not too stiff. Drop into it as many whole strawberries as it will hold, cutting up a few. Stir as you go, mashing slightly. When the cream won't cover one more strawberry, refrigerate it for an hour. It will be a cold, pale pink cream. Crust it over with colored sugar. (One good kind of colored sugar is Tinties, made by Charles Southwell & Co., Ltd., College Street, Ipswich, England. This sugar is sold in fine gourmet shops, including the Old House Epicurean.) Arrange bowl with individual berry dishes on the buffet table.

Escalope of Ham and Eggs

¼ pound (1 stick) butter or margarine	2 tablespoons Worcestershire sauce
4 pounds sliced mushrooms	1 cup chopped parsley
1 cup finely chopped green pepper	6 cans condensed cream of celery soup, undiluted
1 cup finely chopped onion	2 cups light cream
2 tablespoons salt	48 hard-cooked eggs
1 tablespoon coarsely ground black pepper	6 cups cooked ham cubes
	6 cups dry fine bread crumbs

Melt butter, and saute mushrooms, green pepper, and onion until soft but not browned. Add seasonings. Add soup and cream and stir until blended and hot. Slice eggs into sauce and gently fold in. Fold in ham cubes. Pour into several casseroles or 24 individual ramekins. Top with bread crumbs and keep hot in slow oven until needed. *(Makes 24 large servings.)*

Sweet Potato Pone

8 large raw sweet potatoes (enough to make 8 cups), pared and grated	2 cups chopped pecans
	8 eggs, well beaten
	2 cups cream
3 cups sugar	2 cups milk
1 tablespoon nutmeg	¼ pound butter
1 tablespoon salt	

Combine sweet potatoes, sugar, nutmeg, salt, and pecans. Mix well. Combine eggs, cream, and milk. Add to sweet-potato mixture. Pour into a well-buttered 12x12x1-inch baking pan. Dot with butter. Bake at 350 degrees for 45 minutes to 1 hour, or until set. *(Makes 24 servings.)*

Eggplant Pickle

2 large eggplants
¾ cup olive oil
1 clove garlic, crushed
1 cup chopped onion
1 can (1 pound, 13 ounces)
  Italian plum tomatoes
1 cup tomato sauce
2 cups sliced green pepper
2 cups sliced celery
¼ cup chopped parsley

1 teaspoon basil
¼ teaspoon coarsely ground
  black pepper
2 teaspoons salt
2 tablespoons sugar
¼ cup wine vinegar
¼ cup capers
⅔ cup sliced stuffed green
  olives

Cut unpeeled eggplant into 1-inch cubes. Brown in oil. Remove from pan; drain on paper towels. Saute garlic and onion in pan, adding a little more oil if necessary. Add tomatoes and rest of ingredients. Cover and simmer 15 minutes. Remove from heat, add eggplant, and cool. Refrigerate, covered, overnight to blend flavors. *(Makes 24 servings.)*

Honey Nut Coffee Cake

1 pound 4 ounces (5 sticks)
  margarine
4½ cups light brown sugar
9 cups flour
1¾ teaspoons salt
2 teaspoons cinnamon
2 teaspoons nutmeg

1 pound coarsely chopped
  walnuts
1 tablespoon baking soda
5 eggs, slightly beaten
¾ cup honey
3½ cups buttermilk

Cream margarine and sugar until very light and smooth. Combine flour, salt, and spices. Mix well. Add to margarine mixture and mix on low speed in mixer, or with hand beater, until blended and mixture is lumpy.

Add nuts. Mix until just blended. Remove 1 cup of the mixture and set aside for topping. Mix soda into remaining mixture just enough to blend well. Mixture will be fine and crumbly at this stage. Combine eggs, honey, and buttermilk. Mix into dry ingredients by hand, or on low speed of mixer, just until flour is moistened. Spread in greased and floured 18x26-inch loaf pan. Sprinkle with topping. Bake in a 375-degree oven until lightly browned and done, about 35 minutes. *(Makes 24 portions.)*

Spring Bridge Party Luncheon

VIOLET FIZZ
LAVENDER AND OLD LACE

JELLIED CHICKEN SALAD
HOT BLUEBERRY FINGERS

VIOLET ICE CREAM

Violet Fizz

Juice of ½ lemon
1½ ounces dry gin
½ teaspoon confectioners' sugar

½ ounce Crème Yvette
Club soda

Shake all ingredients but soda with cracked ice and strain into 7-ounce highball glass. Fill with soda. This is not only a delicious drink but a beautiful one.

Lavender and Old Lace

⅔ cup grape juice
Juice of 1 lime, or 1 teaspoon
  lime juice

1 tablespoon honey
1 egg white
Club soda

Combine grape juice, honey, and lime juice in a bowl. Beat egg white until stiff but not dry. Add beaten egg white, a small amount at a time, to fruit juices. Pour over ice cubes into highball glass. Fill with soda.

Jellied Chicken Salad

3-ounce package grape-flavored gelatin
1 cup hot water
¼ teaspoon salt
½ cup mayonnaise
Juice of 1 lemon
1 cup diced celery

1½ cups cold cooked chicken, diced
½ cup chopped nuts
½ cup heavy cream, whipped
1 cup fresh grapes, halved and seeded
Lettuce or other salad greens

Dissolve gelatin in hot water. Chill until slightly thickened. Add salt and blend in mayonnaise. Fold in remaining ingredients except greens. Turn into a 1-quart mold and chill. Unmold on greens. *(Makes 8 servings.)*

Hot Blueberry Fingers

2 cups flour
½ cup sugar
2 teaspoons baking powder
½ teaspoon salt
1 cup milk

1 egg, well beaten
4 tablespoons melted butter
1 cup canned blueberries with juice

Mix all ingredients just enough to moisten dry ingredients. Do not beat. Pour batter into well-buttered corn-stick pans, filling them two-thirds full. Bake in a hot oven at 400 degrees for 20 to 25 minutes.

Violet Ice Cream

To 1 pint whipped cream, add 2 pints fine, fresh brown-bread crumbs. Freeze lightly just until set. Beat in 1 cup coarse crystallized sugar or crushed sugar candy (it should be about the texture of fine crushed ice). Put ice cream into a fancy mold or 8 individual molds. Chill thoroughly.

Unmold and cover lavishly with crystallized violets (obtainable at gourmet shops, including the Old House Epicurean). This makes a beautiful dessert. *(Makes 8 servings.)*

Summer Bridge Party Luncheon

STRAWBERRY FIZZ

JELLIED SHRIMP SALAD
WITH TOMATO MAYONNAISE

PINK RICE MUFFINS

MERINGUE ROSES

Strawberry Fizz

2½ cups boiling water
1 tablespoon orange pekoe tea
1 package frozen strawberries,
    sliced and thawed

6-ounce can frozen limeade
    concentrate, undiluted
2 cups club soda, chilled

Pour boiling water over tea. Let steep 5 minutes and then strain. Cool. Add strawberries and limeade concentrate. Chill. Add club soda and serve immediately in highball glasses over ice cubes. Float on top fresh strawberries with stems on, dipped in confectioners' sugar. *(Makes 8 glasses.)*

Jellied Shrimp Salad

1 tablespoon unflavored gelatin
¼ cup cold water
1 cup mayonnaise
½ cup juice drained from sweet
    pickled beets
2 tablespoons lemon juice

2 tablespoons tarragon vinegar
½ teaspoon salt
1 cup cooked or canned shrimp
½ cup diced celery
½ cup diced pickled beets
Salad greens

Soften gelatin in cold water and dissolve over hot water. Add rest of ingredients except greens and chill. When gelatin begins to thicken, stir slightly and pour into individual oiled molds.

Unmold on salad greens and serve with Tomato Mayonnaise. *(Makes 8 servings.)*

Tomato Mayonnaise

1 cup mayonnaise	Grind of fresh black pepper
1 tablespoon tomato paste	¼ teaspoon salt, or more to
2 or 3 drops garlic juice	taste

Mix all ingredients together well.

Pink Rice Muffins

1 cup boiled rice	2 tablespoons grenadine syrup
1 cup milk	1½ cups sifted flour
2 eggs, beaten	½ teaspoon salt
5 tablespoons melted shortening	3 teaspoons baking powder

Beat rice, milk, eggs, and shortening well. Add grenadine and mix. Sift flour, salt, and baking powder into batter. Mix only enough to combine. Pour into greased muffin pan and bake for 25 minutes at 400 degrees. *(Makes 12 muffins.)*

Meringue Roses

4 egg whites	1 tablespoon grenadine
Pinch of salt	¼ teaspoon cream of tartar
4 drops almond extract	1 cup fine sugar

Beat egg whites until stiff but not dry with salt, almond extract, and grenadine. Beat in cream of tartar and sugar a little at a time. Put meringue into a pastry bag and, by forcing it through, make 8 individual shells, about 4 inches in diameter, on a buttered cookie sheet. Force the meringue out in petal shapes around the edges of the shells. Bake for 10 minutes in a slow oven. Lower heat to very slow and continue baking for 20 to 25 minutes longer. Do not let shells brown. Remove from oven and cool. *(Makes 8 shells.)*

When ready to serve, fill shells with strawberry ice cream. You can fill them ahead of time and keep them in the freezer if you wish. Top with whipped cream and sprinkle crystallized rose petals (available in gourmet shops) over the cream.

Fall Bridge Party
Luncheon

GOLDEN DREAM COCKTAIL
GOLDEN CADILLAC

CHICKEN BREASTS VALENCIA
SOUR CREAM CORN STICKS

CHARTREUSE FLOATING ISLAND

Golden Dream Cocktail

1 ounce Galliano liqueur   2 ounces orange juice
1 ounce Cointreau   3 ounces sweet cream

Shake with cracked ice and strain into cocktail glasses.

Golden Cadillac

1½ cups sweetened pineapple   ¼ cup confectioners' sugar
    juice   Lemon peel
Juice of 1 lemon   1 pint softened lemon sherbet

Combine pineapple juice, lemon juice, and sugar. Twist a strip of lemon peel over and add. Blend well. Add lemon sherbet and blend until smooth. Serve in champagne glasses. Garnish with spiral of lemon peel in each glass. *(Makes 8 servings.)*

Chicken Breasts Valencia

8 chicken breasts
1 cup salad oil
4 cloves garlic, minced
2 large onions, chopped
2 green peppers, chopped
2 bay leaves
2 cups whole cooked tomatoes

2 quarts chicken broth (stock made from chicken bouillon cubes will do)
2 tablespoons salt
1 teaspoon powdered saffron
2 cups rice

Brown breasts in oil. Remove breasts and place in a casserole. Saute garlic, onions, and peppers in the hot oil until onions are golden. Add bay leaves and tomatoes, and cook a few minutes longer. Pour over breasts in casserole. Add chicken broth, salt, saffron, and rice. Mix well. Cover casserole and bake at 350 degrees for 20 minutes, or until rice is tender, stirring once or twice. Chicken and rice will be a beautiful golden color. *(Makes 8 servings.)*

Sour Cream Corn Sticks

2 cups yellow cornmeal
2 tablespoons sugar
1 teaspoon salt
1 teaspoon baking powder

1 teaspoon baking soda
2 eggs
2 cups sour cream

Sift dry ingredients together. Beat eggs and add sour cream. Add to dry ingredients and mix well. Pour into greased corn-stick pan and bake at 400 degrees for 30 minutes. *(Makes 12 corn sticks.)*

Chartreuse Floating Island

5 eggs (3 separated)
½ cup plus 6 tablespoons sugar
¼ teaspoon salt

1 quart milk, scalded
2¾ teaspoons yellow chartreuse
Yellow food coloring

Beat 3 egg yolks and 2 whole eggs together slightly. Add ½ cup sugar and salt. Mix and add hot milk gradually, stirring constantly. Cook custard in top of double boiler until it coats spoon, stirring constantly. Add 2 teaspoons chartreuse. Pour into large pan.

Beat remaining egg whites until foamy. Beat in additional 6 tablespoons sugar gradually and a few drops of yellow food coloring. Add ¾ teaspoon yellow chartreuse to meringue, and drop meringue, using large spoon, onto hot custard. Cover pan tightly until mixture is cool, then chill. *(Serves 8.)*

Winter Bridge Party Luncheon

APPLE SNOW

WHITE LADY
HOT CHESTNUT PIE
CELERY LEAF SALAD

ANGEL'S SNOWBALLS

Apple Snow

4 cups cold buttermilk	Sugar to taste (about 4
2 cups chilled applesauce	teaspoons)
1 tablespoon lemon juice	Ground allspice

Mix all ingredients except allspice, which is to be sprinkled over the top. Serve in punch cups or champagne glasses. *(Makes 8 punch cups.)*

White Lady

1 egg white	1 teaspoon sweet cream
1 teaspoon confectioners' sugar	1½ ounces dry gin

Shake with cracked ice and strain into cocktail glass.

Hot Chestnut Pie

4 eggs	1 tablespoon flour
2 cups cream	¼ teaspoon grated nutmeg
1½ tablespoons melted butter	½ teaspoon salt
1 cup roasted chestnuts, peeled and coarsely chopped	Pastry for single 9-inch pie crust
1 pound Swiss cheese, grated	6 slices crisp fried bacon, crumbled
1 large raw onion, sliced	

169

Beat eggs. Add cream and melted butter and mix well. Stir in chestnuts, Swiss cheese, and onion. Mix in flour, nutmeg, and salt. Pour into unbaked pie shell. Sprinkle a few chopped chestnuts and bacon crumbs on top. Bake at 375 degrees for about 45 minutes, or until custard is set and top is browned. Serve warm. *(Makes 8 servings.)*

Celery Leaf Salad

4 cups celery-top leaves, torn
2 cans (5 ounces each) water chestnuts, drained and thinly sliced
4 tablespoons chopped parsley
4 tablespoons minced onions
1 cup diced green pepper

2 cups shredded fresh spinach leaves
4 teaspoons caraway seeds
2 cups bottled Old House Salad Dressing (or any good thick salad dressing)

Toss all together with dressing and serve immediately. *(Makes 8 servings.)*

Angel's Snow Balls

2 cups sugar
1 cup water
32 marshmallows
4 egg whites

1½ cups candied or crystallized angelica
1 quart pistachio ice cream
Shredded coconut

Boil sugar and water together for 5 minutes. Cut marshmallows into small pieces and add to hot syrup. Stir until dissolved and pour mixture gradually over stiffly beaten egg whites. Beat until smooth and well blended. Stir in 1 cup angelica (can be found at gourmet shops). *(Makes 5 cups sauce.)*

Scoop ice cream and roll into balls. Quickly roll ice cream balls in coconut. Put marshmallow-angelica sauce in the bottom of sherbet dishes. Place a coconut ice cream ball on top of sauce and sprinkle all with remaining crystallized angelica.

Keep in freezer until needed. The cold sherbet glasses will keep the snowballs from melting too soon after being served. *(Makes 8 snowballs.)*

Poker Party

OPENING COCKTAIL

MONTE CARLO IMPERIAL HIGHBALL
MOLDED CHEESE SALAD
BAKED BEANS FULL HOUSE
STEAK AND KIDNEY PIES

FRIED APPLE PIES
EMPEROR FRANZ JOSEF'S MOCHA AND RUM

❋ *Poker Party*

This menu is very elegant, in contrast to the usual poker-party fare of cold cuts, rye bread, and cheese. It is easily prepared ahead and arranged on a buffet or side table for the men to enjoy whenever they desire. Every man there will envy the host for his clever and considerate wife!

Opening Cocktail

½ ounce grenadine   1½ ounces bourbon whiskey
½ ounce Italian vermouth

Stir with cracked ice and strain into cocktail glass.

Monte Carlo Imperial Highball

2 ounces dry gin   Juice of ¼ lemon
½ ounce white crème de menthe   Champagne

Shake gin, liqueur, and lemon juice with cracked ice and strain into highball glass. Fill glass with champagne.

Molded Cheese Salad

2 packages (6 ounces each)
  lemon gelatin
3 cups boiling water
3 cups cottage cheese
1 cup grated sharp cheese
½ cup green onions, chopped
  with tops

2 tablespoons chopped green
  pepper
3 tablespoons chopped
  cucumber
½ cup lemon juice
1 cup mayonnaise

Dissolve gelatin in boiling water and cool. Stir in remaining ingredients. Pour into individual molds and chill until firm. For buffet style, pour into one large fancy mold. Serve with Old House Salad Dressing (or any good thick dressing) on lettuce. *(Makes 8 servings.)*

Baked Beans Full House

1 pound bacon
15½-ounce can kidney beans
15-ounce can lima beans
16-ounce can pork and beans
1 cup tomato puree
1 cup finely chopped onions

½ cup dark brown sugar
2 tablespoons honey
2 tablespoons dry mustard
2 teaspoons salt
½ teaspoon coarsely ground
  black pepper

Fry all but 4 or 5 strips bacon until crisp; drain and crumble. Drain liquid from beans. Mix beans with other ingredients. Put in a greased casserole. Cover with 4 or 5 strips bacon and bake at 350 degrees for 1 hour. These are good hot or cold. *(Makes 8 servings.)*

Steak and Kidney Pies

2 pounds beef chuck
1 pound lamb kidneys
Flour
Bacon drippings
1 large onion, coarsely chopped
1 cup sliced mushrooms
1 cup hot water

½ cup Worcestershire sauce
1 teaspoon salt
¼ teaspoon coarsely ground
  black pepper
Pastry for double 9-inch pie
  crust

Cut beef into 1-inch cubes. Cut kidneys lengthwise, then across into cubes. Soak kidneys 10 minutes in ice water, then drain. Dredge meat in flour and brown in a skillet with bacon drippings. Remove meat to a kettle and cook onion in the skillet until soft but not browned. Pour onion and drippings

172

into kettle with beef and kidneys. Add rest of ingredients and simmer, covered, until meat is tender.

Gravy should be thick. If not, mix a little flour with enough water to make a smooth paste and stir into gravy. Cook a few minutes longer. Pour into individual ovenproof dishes or ramekins and top with a flaky crust. Bake in a 450-degree oven until crust is nicely browned. These are as good cold as they are hot — therefore they can be made ahead and served whenever desired. *(Makes 8 servings.)*

Fried Apple Pies

2 cups flour	¼ teaspoon cinnamon
1 teaspoon salt	¼ teaspoon nutmeg
½ cup shortening	1 cup slivered blanched almonds
⅓ cup ice water	
2 cups thick applesauce, sweetened to taste	

Sift flour and salt together. Cut in shortening and mix with hands. Add water. Roll out about ⅛-inch thick on a floured board. Cut out rounds about 4 or 5 inches in diameter. (An empty coffee can makes a good cutter.) Mix applesauce, spices, and almonds.

In each round, place 2 tablespoons applesauce mixture. Moisten edges of pastry with cold water. Fold each round to make a semicircle and press edges together with a fork dipped in cold water. Fry in deep fat until golden brown. Drain on paper and sprinkle with a mixture of cinnamon, nutmeg, and confectioners' sugar. May be served either hot or cold. *(Makes 8 pies.)*

Emperor Franz Josef's Mocha and Rum
After an evening of cards, the Austrian emperor always enjoyed having this stimulating drink served to him and his entourage at the royal palace.

2 cups strong coffee	4 tablespoons sugar
3 cups hot milk	Dark rum
4 ounces cooking chocolate	Whipped cream

Strain coffee and mix it with 2 cups milk. Dissolve chocolate and sugar in 1 cup milk. Stir chocolate mixture into coffee. This can be beaten until frothy and served hot with 1 ounce dark rum added to each cup and topped with whipped cream. Or it may be stored in a pitcher in the refrigerator and served cold in goblets with rum and whipped cream. Either way is delicious.

Teen-Agers' Party

"CHAMPAGNE" COCKTAIL
CARDINAL PUNCH

BURGER BAKE STROGANOFF
MOLDED WALDORF SALAD
PEANUT BUNS

FUNNY CAKE
WITH CHOCOLATE, BUTTERSCOTCH, OR ORANGE SAUCE
ROSY CINNAMON APPLES

"Champagne" Cocktail

2 dashes bitters
1 lump sugar
Pomac or sparkling Catabaw
juice (nonalcoholic)

Spiral rind of ½ lemon

Pour bitters on sugar lump, add ice cubes, and fill glass with Pomac. (Pomac is a delicious nonalcoholic sparkling beverage, obtainable in most chain stores.) Add lemon rind.

Cardinal Punch

Juice of 1 dozen lemons
Enough confectioners' sugar to
    sweeten
2 quarts cranberry juice cocktail

½ pint sweet vermouth
1 quart sparkling Catabaw juice
    (nonalcoholic)

Mix lemon juice and sugar well, then pour over large block of ice in a punch bowl. Add rest of ingredients. Stir and float frozen sliced strawberries and paper-thin slices of lemon in the punch. *(Makes 25 punch cups.)*

Burger Bake Stroganoff

4 teaspoons rosemary
8 bay leaves, crumbled
1 gallon cold water
1 tablespoon salt
6 cups uncooked elbow
   macaroni
5 pounds ground beef
6 cups chopped onions
2 cups capers
1 cup milk

4 cans condensed cream of
   mushroom soup, undiluted
1 cup tomato ketchup
1½ tablespoons salt
1 teaspoon coarsely ground
   black pepper
1 quart sour cream
Paprika as needed
½ cup chopped parsley

Tie rosemary and bay leaves in a cheesecloth bag and add to water. Bring to a boil. Add 1 tablespoon salt and macaroni. Cook until tender, remove bag, and drain macaroni.

Brown meat and onions, cooking and stirring until meat is broken up and onions are soft. Pour off fat. Blend in capers, milk, soup, ketchup, remaining salt, pepper, and sour cream. Fold in macaroni. Turn into a 12x20x2½-inch baking pan. Sprinkle generously with paprika. Bake at 350 degrees for 30 minutes, or until hot and bubbly. Garnish with parsley. *(Makes 24 servings.)*

Molded Waldorf Salad

4 packages (12 ounces) lemon
   gelatin
1 quart boiling water
1 quart ice water
2 tablespoons lemon juice
1 tablespoon sugar
¼ teaspoon salt

3 cups peeled, diced apples
3 cups diced celery
½ pound chopped dates
1 cup chopped maraschino
   cherries
½ pound chopped nuts

Dissolve gelatin in boiling water. Add ice water and stir. Add lemon juice, sugar, and salt. Pour gelatin into two 10x3½x2½-inch loaf pans. Chill until slightly thickened. Stir in apples, celery, dates, cherries, and nuts. Chill until firm. Cut loaves into 12 portions each. Arrange squares on greens on a large tray. *(Makes 24 servings.)*

Peanut Buns

2 cups milk
1 cake yeast
¼ cup sugar
8 cups sifted flour
2 eggs

1 teaspoon salt
⅓ cup softened butter
2 cups peanuts, coarsely
  chopped

Scald milk and cool to lukewarm. Add yeast and let soften. Add sugar and 4 cups flour to make a sponge. Beat well. Cover and let rise in warm place until doubled in bulk, about 1½ hours. Add unbeaten eggs, salt, and butter. Mix thoroughly until blended. Sift remaining flour over nuts and mix well. Add to first mixture and work to a smooth, elastic dough. Cover and let rise to double in bulk, about 1½ hours. Turn onto floured board and shape into buns. Place on baking sheet an inch apart. Let rise until light, then bake at 375 degrees 20 minutes. *(Makes 30 buns.)*

Funny Cake

9 cups plain cake mix
4 cups sugar
3 cups milk
6 eggs, or enough to make 1¼
  cups
1 tablespoon vanilla

1 cup chopped nuts
1 cup shredded coconut
6 unbaked 9-inch pie shells of
  rich pastry dough for deep-
  dish pies, with high fluted rims

Combine all cake ingredients in a mixing bowl and beat at low speed until batter is smooth. Pour batter into unbaked pie shells, dividing it equally among the 6 and leaving room for your favorite sauce on top, about ½ inch. Carefully pour lukewarm sauce over batter, allowing about 1 cup sauce per cake. Sprinkle with nuts and coconut. Bake at 350 degrees 50 to 60 minutes. Served topped with whipped cream or ice cream. Cut cakes into quarters. *(Makes 24 servings.)*

Sauces for Funny Cake
Chocolate Sauce — the all-time favorite

6 ounces unsweetened chocolate
3 cups water
4 cups sugar

1½ cups (3 sticks) butter or
  margarine
2 tablespoons vanilla

Combine chocolate and water. Cook over low heat, stirring until chocolate is melted. Add sugar; stir constantly until mixture comes to a boil. Remove from heat. Add butter and vanilla. Stir until blended.

Butterscotch Sauce

1½ cups (3 sticks) butter
3 cups brown sugar, firmly
  packed

1 cup light corn syrup
1¼ cups water
1 tablespoon vanilla

Combine butter, brown sugar, syrup, and water. Cook over low heat, stirring constantly, until mixture comes to a boil. Boil 2 minutes. Remove from heat and stir in vanilla.

Orange Sauce

3½ cups orange juice
4½ cups sugar
6 ounces (1½ sticks) butter or
  margarine

2 tablespoons grated orange
  rind

Combine 1½ cups orange juice and sugar. Cook over low heat, stirring constantly, until mixture comes to a boil. Boil 1 minute. Remove from heat; stir in remaining 2 cups orange juice, butter, and grated orange rind.

Rosy Cinnamon Apples

24 apples
2 quarts water
4 cups sugar
2 lemons, thinly sliced
1 teaspoon red food coloring

½ cup red-hot cinnamon
  candies
1½ pounds cream cheese
Honey as needed
24 walnut halves

Core and pare apples. Combine water, sugar, lemon slices, red food coloring, and candies. Bring to a boil, stirring until sugar and candies dissolve. Simmer apples in syrup until tender and red, turning often. Drain; chill. Soften cream cheese with honey and stuff apples. Garnish with a walnut-half on top. *(Makes 24 servings.)*

Japanese Party

SAKE
OKI SUKI

JAPANESE SALAD
IMPERIAL PORK SALAD
TSUGARU
WITH MUSTARD SAUCE
MANJU
JAPANESE SAVORY RICE
SNOW PEAS WITH BEEF

JASMINE TEA AND FORTUNE COOKIES

❋ *Japanese Party*

To create an atmosphere for this festivity, decorate the room with Japanese lanterns, floor pillows to sit or kneel on, low tables, and hibachis, either to prepare the food at the tables or to keep the prepared food warm until served. Women should wear long kimonos, white socks, sandals, sashes with huge butterfly bows in back, flowers in their hair, and should carry fans. For the men, short kimonos, with knee-length or long trousers, and sandals. Chopsticks for those who are adept.

Sake

A rice wine served in tiny cups, either chilled or at room temperature.

Oki Suki

2 lobster tails (8 ounces each), shelled and cut bite-size
1 pound fresh shrimp, shelled and cleaned
½ pound red snapper fillet, cut bite-size
½ pound fresh scallops
12 cherrystone clams or oysters, shelled
½ pound king crab legs, cut bite-size
½ bunch green onions, cut lengthwise
¼ stalk celery cabbage, cut in 1-inch pieces
1 cup yam noodles (shirataki) or regular noodles
½ cup canned bamboo shoots, drained and sliced ¼-inch thick
6 large mushrooms
3 cups chicken bouillon
¼ cup sake (rice wine)
2 teaspoons salt
1 teaspoon soy sauce
Pinch Japanese pepper (sansho)

If you are bringing the seafood and vegetables to the table to be cooked, arrange them attractively on a large platter. Combine bouillon, wine, and seasonings in a pot or deep chafing dish. Bring to a boil. Add ingredients from platter a few at a time. Simmer uncovered until cooked. Serve with hot steamed rice. *(Makes 6 servings.)*

Japanese Salad

1 head lettuce
2 large cucumbers
2 large turnips
2 tablespoons celery salt

Shred lettuce. Peel cucumbers and turnips, and slice paper thin lengthwise. Sprinkle with celery salt and leave 2 days. No need to use any other dressing. Toss together and chill.

Imperial Pork Salad

1 head lettuce, shredded
2 cups shredded celery cabbage
½ cup chopped parsley
⅔ cup oil
⅔ cup red wine vinegar
2 tablespoons soy sauce
2 teaspoons dry mustard
1 teaspoon seasoned salt
⅛ teaspoon pepper
½ pound (1 cup) cooked diced pork
½ cup sesame seeds, lightly toasted

Combine lettuce, celery cabbage, and parsley in salad bowl. To prepare sauce, combine oil, vinegar, soy sauce, mustard, seasoned salt, and pepper in blazer or chafing dish. Bring to a boil; cook 2 minutes. Add pork; heat through. To serve, turn the very hot sauce into the salad bowl; toss quickly. Sprinkle each portion with sesame seeds and serve at once. *(Makes 6 servings.)*

Tsugaru

2 pounds highly spiced pork sausage	2 eggs
	½ cup chopped onions
2 cups finely chopped apples	2 teaspoons dried parsley flakes

Combine all ingredients; shape into small patties and grill on medium heat. Serve with Mustard Sauce. *(Makes 6 servings.)*

Mustard Sauce

1 cup dry mustard	Beer
1 tablespoon sesame or safflower oil	

Mix mustard and oil, and add enough beer to make sauce desired consistency, either thick or thin. Mix until smooth.

Manju

SHIROAN:

6 cups cooked or canned lima beans	2 cups sugar
	¼ cup honey

Drain beans and mash. Add sugar and honey to mashed beans. Cook and stir over low heat until thickened. Form into balls 1-inch thick.

PASTRY:

4 cups flour	4 large eggs, lightly beaten
2 cups sugar	½ cup milk
2½ teaspoons baking powder	Shiroan
1 teaspoon salt	Poppy seeds
⅓ cup shortening	

Sift flour, sugar, baking powder, and salt together. Cut in shortening. Combine 3 eggs and milk; add to flour mixture; mix to form stiff dough. Roll out on floured waxed paper; cut in size to wrap around shiroan balls. Brush top of filled pastries with remaining beaten egg; sprinkle with poppy seeds. Bake at 400 degrees for about 15 minutes. *(Makes about 60 pastries.)*

Japanese Savory Rice

1 cup canned bamboo shoots, drained	½ pound (1 cup) chopped cooked chicken
2 pounds fresh mushrooms or 1 cup canned mushrooms, drained	2 cups boiled rice
	½ teaspoon sugar
	1 cup chicken bouillon or stock
¼ cup (1 stick) butter	1½ teaspoons soy sauce

Slice bamboo shoots and mushrooms thinly and fry in butter for 2 minutes. Add chopped chicken, mushrooms, and bamboo shoots to the rice. Add sugar and stock, and stir gently. Cover pan and simmer very gently for 30 minutes, until stock is absorbed. Stir in soy sauce and serve hot. *(Makes 6 servings.)*

Snow Peas with Beef

1½ pounds beef tenderloin, sliced thin	4 cups chicken bouillon or stock
Peanut oil as needed	1 teaspoon sorghum molasses
Salt to taste	½ pound snow peas
4 tablespoons cornstarch	1 cup sliced water chestnuts

Saute beef in peanut oil. Season with salt. Blend cornstarch with chicken stock. Add to meat; add remaining ingredients. Cook until sauce thickens and clears. Adjust seasonings to taste. *(Makes 6 servings.)*

Jasmine Tea and Fortune Cookies

In the Orient, green (unfermented) and oolong (semifermented) teas are preferred. They are delicate, with pleasing aromas. The best one is jasmine tea—oolong leaves scented with jasmine petals. No cream, sugar, or lemon is served with jasmine tea. Serve in tiny cups. Have plates of fortune cookies on the side. (Fortune cookies are available in gourmet shops.)

Hawaiian Luau

WAHINE
BABALU

HUNAHUNANUKANUKAPUA
POLYNESIAN CHICKEN
OUTRIGGER RIBS
COCONUT SALAD
BAKED BANANAS

KONA
GINGER HAWAIIAN PIE

❋ *Hawaiian Luau*

In preparing to attend a luau, women should wear grass skirts and flowered bras, or brightly flowered muumuus (baggy shifts); flowers behind their ears, flower garlands around neck, arms, and ankles. Men can wear bright flowered shirts and shorts. Everybody barefoot!

Wahine (Wa-hee-nee)

1½ ounces unsweetened
   pineapple juice
1 ounce white rum
1 ounce vodka

½ ounce lemon juice
¼ ounce bar syrup (3 cups
   sugar and 1 cup water boiled
   for 5 minutes)

Combine all ingredients with 1 cup shaved ice in a blender or bowl. Cover and blend, or beat with hand beater. Pour into a glass over ice cubes. Garnish with a pineapple wedge, a cherry, and a sprig of mint.

Babalu

¾ ounce grapefruit-pineapple frozen juice concentrate, undiluted

2 ounces golden rum
½ ounce lemon juice

Put all ingredients and 1 cup shaved ice in a blender or bowl. Cover and blend, or beat with hand beater. Pour over ice cubes in a tall glass. Garnish with a cherry, a pineapple wedge, and a sprig of mint.

Hunahunanukanukapua
A tiny fish, not as long as its name!

2 pounds fresh smelts or fresh sardines
Enough flour to roll cleaned fish in
Fat for frying
1 carrot, diced
1 onion, chopped
4 cloves garlic, chopped

½ cup salad oil
1 cup tarragon vinegar
1 teaspoon seasoned salt
⅛ teaspoon coarsely ground black pepper
⅛ teaspoon thyme
1 bay leaf, crumbled
Chopped parsley

Roll fish in flour and fry in deep fat until golden brown. Saute carrot, onion, and garlic in salad oil until soft. Add rest of ingredients except parsley and simmer for 10 minutes. Pour marinade over fish and let stand overnight before serving. Serve cold. Garnish with parsley. *(Makes 12 servings.)*

Polynesian Chicken

6 fresh pineapples
½ pound (2 sticks) butter
1 cup flour
6 cups chicken stock or bouillon
3 cups cream
¾ cup dry sherry
¾ cup Cointreau
3 cups cooked cubed chicken

2 cups sliced fresh mushrooms or 1 cup canned mushrooms, drained
3 cups unsweetened shredded coconut
3 cups sliced toasted almonds
12 cups cooked rice
1-pound jar chutney

Split pineapples in half lengthwise; hollow out, leaving half of fruit in shell. Score fruit left in shell and loosen, leaving in place in shell. Chop pineapple removed from shell.

Cream butter and flour together. Add chicken stock, chopped pineapple, and cream. Simmer until thickened. Add sherry, Cointreau, cubed chicken, and mushrooms. Simmer 10 minutes. Adjust seasoning to taste.

Turn mixture into pineapple halves on top of loosened fruit. Arrange shells on a baking sheet and bake at 350 degrees for 45 minutes. Sprinkle top with coconut and almonds, and bake until coconut and almonds are browned. Serve with cooked rice and chutney on the side. *(Makes 12 servings.)*

Outrigger Ribs

10 pounds lean, meaty spareribs	1 cup soy sauce
3½ cups crushed pineapple	½ cup Worcestershire sauce
½ cup horseradish mustard	1 tablespoon seasoned salt
1 cup lemon juice	1 teaspoon pepper

Arrange ribs in a baking pan. Roast at 325 degrees for 1½ hours. Pour off fat. Combine remaining ingredients and pour over ribs. Roast 45 minutes longer, turning ribs two or three times in sauce. *(Makes 12 servings)*.

Coconut Salad

Take 6 fresh, slightly green coconuts, remove coconut meat from shells, and shred as for cabbage slaw. Serve well tossed with French dressing. *(Makes 12 servings.)*

Baked Bananas

Bake 1 dozen firm, slightly green bananas with skins on at 325 degrees for 30 minutes, or until a fork pierces them easily. To serve, slit skin, sprinkle with a bit of salt and lime juice. Serve hot in skins.

Kona

1 quart coconut ice cream	6 bananas
12 slices pineapple (fresh or canned)	2 cups apricot preserves
	1 cup white rum

Mound ice cream on pineapple slices, and slice bananas over top. Blend apricot preserves with enough rum to thin sauce to pouring consistency. Spoon over ice cream and fruits. *(Makes 12 servings.)*

Serve iced Hawaiian coffee sweetened with heavy rum, and pass sliced preserved ginger with it.

Ginger Hawaiian Pie

2 tablespoons unflavored gelatin
½ cup cold water
1⅓ cups sugar
½ tablespoon ground ginger
½ teaspoon ground mace
6 egg yolks, beaten
2 cups crushed pineapple with juice
½ cup lemon juice
1 tablespoon grated lemon rind
½ teaspoon salt
6 egg whites
2 baked pie shells (9 inches each)
1 cup whipping cream
½ cup toasted coconut

Soften gelatin in cold water. Mix ⅔ cup sugar and spices; add egg yolks, pineapple, and lemon juice. Cook over hot water, stirring until thickened. Remove from heat. Stir in gelatin and grated lemon rind. Chill until slightly thickened.

Add salt to egg whites. Beat until foamy. Add ⅓ cup sugar gradually, beating until stiff, glossy peaks form. Fold into gelatin mixture. Turn into baked pie shells. Chill until firm. Whip cream, sweeten with ⅓ cup sugar, and spread on pies. Sprinkle with coconut. *(Makes two 9-inch pies.)*

Mexican Fiesta

MARGARITA
MEXITINI
NACHOS

TAMALE HORS D'OEUVRE

BEEF PICADILLO
CHILI CON QUESO
GUACAMOLE
FRIJOLES
CHICKEN TAMALE PIE

TORTILLAS
NATILLAS
FLAMING BANDERA

❋ Mexican Fiesta

Ask your guests to come in Mexican or Spanish attire: full skirts, off-shoulder blouses, fans, and mantillas for the women. Spanish shawls, by all means! For the men, bright-colored sashes, serapes over the shoulder, mustachios. And, of course, bring guitars.

Margarita

1 ounce lime or lemon juice   ½ ounce Triple Sec or
½ ounce tequila   Cointreau

Moisten rim of cocktail glass with fruit rind. Spin moist rim in salt. Shake ingredients with cracked ice and strain into glass.

Mexitini

3 ounces tequila   **½ ounce dry vermouth**

Shake with cracked ice and strain into cocktail glass. Serve with a small whole green cocktail pepper.

Nachos

1 pound sharp cheese   **Large corn chips**
Light cream
1 cup chopped jalapenos (hot peppers available canned in gourmet shops)

Soften cheese with cream to spreading consistency. Add peppers and mix well. Chill until firm. Put ½ teaspoon of cheese-pepper mixture on each corn chip. Put chips on baking sheet and broil 1 minute.

Tamale Hors d'Oeuvre

Peel corn shucks from canned tamales. Cut tamales into pieces 1-inch long. Dip into beaten egg, then yellow cornmeal, and fry in deep hot fat. Serve hot with toothpicks and a hot chili sauce to which chili pepper has been added to taste. (Some people like it hotter than others).

Beef Picadillo

1 pound ground beef   **1½ cups toasted sliced almonds**
1 pound ground pork   **5 cloves garlic, minced**
2 teaspoons salt   **2 cans (6 ounces each) tomato**
½ teaspoon black pepper   **paste**
6 peeled chopped tomatoes   **4 chopped jalapenos**
6 chopped green onions with   **1½ cups seedless raisins**
tops   **½ teaspoon oregano**
6 diced potatoes   **Tostados (Mexican tortillas**
1½ cups diced red pimientos   **available at gourmet shops)**

Mix meat well and season with salt and pepper. Add enough water to barely cover and simmer 30 minutes. Add rest of ingredients except tostados and cook until potatoes are done but not mushy. Drain off excess liquid. Serve hot in a chafing dish with tostados. *(Makes 12 servings.)*

Chili Con Queso

4 hot chili peppers, diced
4 green peppers, chopped
2 small onions, chopped fine
4 cups canned tomatoes, drained
4 cups tomato juice

2 small cloves garlic, mashed
4 tablespoons cornstarch
1 pound Monterrey cheese, cut
  in 1-inch pieces

Boil chili peppers, green peppers, onion, tomatoes, and tomato juice together for 15 minutes. Add garlic. Dissolve cornstarch in cold water and blend slowly into mixture. When it thickens, add cheese pieces. Serve on cocktail tortillas. *(Makes 12 servings.)*

Guacamole

6 avocados (very ripe), peeled
  and seeded
2 large peeled tomatoes
2 teaspoons chili powder

2 green peppers, finely chopped
1 large onion, finely chopped
French dressing

Mash avocados and mix with other ingredients. Stir in a small amount of well-seasoned French dressing and serve in lettuce cups.

Frijoles *(Boiled black beans)*

2 pounds dried black beans
½ pound salt pork
Salt to taste
2 pounds tomatoes, peeled and
  quartered

2 large onions, sliced
2 tablespoons chili powder
2 tablespoons black treacle
  (black molasses)

Soak beans overnight with just enough water to barely cover them. Next morning, cut salt pork into 1-inch cubes and cook with beans in same water in which they were soaked until beans are tender. They should be cooked down fairly dry. Adjust with salt to taste. Mix beans with tomatoes, onions, and chili powder. Put bean mixture into a well-greased casserole. Warm black treacle or black molasses in 2 cups warm water and pour over beans. Bake covered in a slow oven for 2 hours. *(Makes 12 servings.)*

Chicken Tamale Pie

6 cups cornmeal mush
6 cups sliced cooked chicken
   (canned boned chicken is
   fine)
2 cups tomato sauce
2 cups whole-kernel corn
4 tablespoons sugar
4 tablespoons oil

½ cup seedless raisins, chopped
24 large stuffed olives, sliced
2 large onions, chopped
2 tablespoons chili powder
½ teaspoon basil
1 pound grated Monterrey
   cheese
Salt and pepper to taste

To prepare cornmeal mush, cook 1 cup dry yellow cornmeal in 6 cups boiling water with 2½ teaspoons salt. Spread cornmeal mush in a greased baking pan or casserole. Arrange sliced chicken over mush. Sprinkle with salt and pepper.

Combine remaining ingredients, except cheese, to make a sauce. Adjust seasoning of sauce with salt and pepper to taste. Pour over chicken. Sprinkle cheese on top. Bake at 350 degrees for 45 minutes. Serve from casserole. *(Makes 12 servings.)*

Tortillas

The staple food of the Mexican people is the tortilla, a flat cake made of cornmeal. One of the most characteristic of all Mexican sounds, as universal as the silvery chime of the church bells, is the quick pat-pat of the women's hands as they shape the moist meal into cakes for frying. Let your guests have the fun of making their own tortillas for dinner. Here is a simple recipe:

12 cups maize or dried yellow
   cornmeal

4 ounces slaked lime (available
   at pharmacies)

Soak maize and slaked lime in enough water to cover for 12 hours. Simmer in same water until tender. Drain and rinse maize well. Pound into a smooth paste. Give each of your guests a ball of paste the size of a large walnut. They should toss and pat it between the palms of their hands with a short, quick motion. As the paste flattens out, it will make a staccato slapping sound. It should be patted, slapped, and stretched until it is very thin; then it is ready to fry on a hot ungreased griddle placed on a charcoal hibachi or grill.

Natillas *(Custard with caramel sauce)*

8 cups milk	12 egg yolks, beaten slightly
1 cup sugar	2 teaspoons vanilla
1 cup sifted flour	1 cup light brown sugar
½ teaspoon salt	

Scald 6 cups milk in top of double boiler. Mix sugar, flour, and salt, and stir in 2 cups cold milk and egg yolks; add mixture to scalded milk. Continue cooking over boiling water, stirring constantly until thick. Remove from heat, let stand a few minutes, then stir in vanilla.

Pour custard into a shallow baking dish. When custard is cold, sprinkle brown sugar generously over top. (Be sure there are no lumps in sugar.) Place baking dish under broiler until all sugar on top has caramelized. Chill several hours in refrigerator so that caramelized sugar forms a sauce on top of custard. *(Makes 12 servings.)*

Flaming Bandera *(After-dinner drink)*

⅓ grenadine
⅓ white crème de cacao
Not quite ⅓ green crème de
    menthe
About 1 teaspoon green
    chartreuse

This drink reproduces the colors of the Mexican flag: red, white, and green. Use 1-ounce pony glasses or cordial glasses, and pour in liqueurs in order given. Float the bit of green chartreuse on top and ignite it.

Roman Party

HOT SPICED CHIANTI
LAURINO
PESTO

LASAGNE
SHRIMP POLENTA
ZUCCHINI SALAD

CASSATA

❋ Roman Party

Just for fun, persuade your guests to come dressed as Roman senators and their ladies, wearing homemade togas, sandals, and olive wreaths.

Hot Spiced Chianti

1 quart Chianti	8 sticks cinnamon
2 oranges, sliced with peel	12 whole cloves
2 lemons, sliced with peel	

Place fruit and spices in wine while it is cold, and heat to a point just below boiling. Serve in Italian pottery mugs. *(Makes 6 servings.)*

Laurino

1 part Campari bitters	1 slice lemon
2 parts sweet vermouth	1 slice orange

Serve in small tumbler with ice.

Pesto

8 anchovy fillets, chopped
¼ pound grated Parmesan
  cheese
½ cup walnuts, chopped fine

1 clove garlic, chopped fine
⅛ teaspoon olive oil
Toasted garlic rounds

Put all ingredients in a bowl. Beat with a wooden spoon or mortar and pestle until they form a smooth paste. Serve thinly spread on toasted garlic rounds.

Lasagne

1 pound lasagne (wide noodles)
2 cups (about 1 pound) ground
  lean beef
3 eggs
2 cloves garlic (1 minced)
2 tablespoons chopped parsley
4 tablespoons grated Parmesan
  cheese
2 tablespoons butter
3 cups stewed or canned
  tomatoes

½ can tomato paste
1 bay leaf
1 teaspoon Jane's Crazy Mixed-
  up Salt (an herbed seasoned
  salt obtained at gourmet
  shops)
⅛ teaspoon coarsely ground
  black pepper
Mozzarella cheese
Salami slices

Cook lasagne in boiling salted water until tender. Drain. Combine beef, eggs, minced garlic, parsley, and 2 tablespoons Parmesan cheese, and form into tiny balls. Saute in butter with whole garlic clove until meatballs are browned on all sides. Remove garlic clove. Add tomatoes, tomato paste, bay leaf, salt, and pepper.

Simmer sauce and meatballs 2 hours. Remove bay leaf. Into a baking dish, pour 1 cup tomato sauce in which meatballs were cooked. On this arrange a layer of noodles, 1 slice mozzarella cheese, a layer of meatballs, and tiny thin slices of salami. Repeat layers until all ingredients are used; the top layer should be tomato sauce. Sprinkle top generously with remaining grated Parmesan cheese. Bake at 350 degrees for 30 minutes, or until bubbling. *(Makes 6 servings.)*

192

Shrimp Polenta

1½ cups semolina, maize, or cornmeal
1 quart boiling water
6 slices breakfast bacon
4 tablespoons condensed tomato puree
4 large onions, chopped

½ pound medium-size mushrooms, sliced (drained, if using canned)
2 cups cooked, diced ham
Salt and pepper
1 cup water
4 cups cooked, cleaned shrimp

Pour semolina into boiling water and cook slowly until thick. Set aside.
Chop bacon and fry lightly. Add tomato puree, onions, mushrooms, and ham. Add salt and pepper to taste. Add 1 cup water, stir and simmer 10 minutes. Fill a buttered casserole and alternate layers of semolina, tomato mixture, and then shrimps. Cover casserole and bake at 350 degrees for 45 minutes. *(Makes 12 servings.)*

Zucchini Salad

Cut up small zucchinis, unpeeled, into rounds about ¼-inch thick. Blanch slices in boiling salt water for about 10 minutes. Remove slices, drain, and dry.

Make a vinaigrette sauce in the proportions of 1 tablespoon tarragon vinegar to 3 tablespoons olive oil. Add chopped parsley, chervil, watercress, chives, and burnet. Make enough sauce to cover zucchini slices. Sprinkle with salt and pepper. Chill and marinate zucchini several hours before serving. Serve with chopped hard-boiled eggs sprinkled on top. *(Makes 6 servings.)*

Cassata

4 egg yolks, beaten
1 cup light cream
½ cup sugar
1 strip lemon peel, chopped

½ cup mixed candied cherries, angelica, candied orange or grapefruit peel, and walnuts, finely chopped

Put egg yolks in double boiler with cream. Cook very slowly, stirring constantly, until mixture thickens. Add sugar and chopped lemon peel during cooking. Cool and add other ingredients. Freeze. *(Makes 6 servings.)*

Paris Left=Bank Party

DUBONNET COCKTAIL
VERMOUTH CASSIS
AMER PICON COCKTAIL

FRENCH ONION TART
COQ AU VIN A LA OLD HOUSE
FRENCH SALAD
THE LONG FRENCH LOAF

TUTTI-FRUTTI FLAMBE

❋ Paris Left-Bank Party

Berets, smocks, baggy trousers, striped turtleneck sweaters, scarves, caps, mustaches, goatees, and beards are the order of the evening for an occasion of this kind. Paintbrushes and palettes are an asset to these costumes.

The following dinner should be accompanied by a good dry red wine.

Dubonnet Cocktail

1½ ounces Dubonnet   1 dash orange bitters
¾ ounce dry gin

Stir with cracked ice and strain into cocktail glass. Twist a strip of lemon peel over top and drop in glass.

Vermouth Cassis

¾ ounce crème de cassis   Club soda
1½ ounces dry vermouth

Put crème de cassis and vermouth in 8-ounce highball glass, add 1 ice cube, fill glass with soda, and stir.

Amer Picon Cocktail

> Juice of 1 lime
> 1 teaspoon grenadine
> 1½ ounces Amer Picon

Shake well with cracked ice and strain into cocktail glass.

French Onion Tart

Line a pie pan with pastry; into pastry slice 1 large Bermuda onion. Over onion pour 2 eggs beaten with ½ cup milk and 1 cup grated Swiss cheese. Sprinkle with salt and pepper. Bake at 400 degrees for 25 or 30 minutes. Cut into narrow wedges to serve.

Coq au Vin à la Old House

> 3 tablespoons butter
> ½ cup diced salt pork
> 1 large Bermuda onion, sliced
> 1 clove garlic, chopped fine
> 2 young chickens (3 pounds each), cut into serving pieces
> 1 tablespoon chopped parsley
> 1 bay leaf
> 1 teaspoon thyme
> 1 teaspoon tarragon
> 1 cup sliced mushrooms
> 2 cups good red wine

Heat butter in an earthenware pot or Dutch oven; add salt pork and onion. When onion is nicely browned, put in garlic and chicken. Add rest of ingredients, except wine. Saute until chicken is golden. Add wine. Cover and cook until chicken is tender. When chicken is done, thicken sauce with 1 tablespoon flour kneaded with 1 tablespoon butter and a little brandy. Pour sauce over chicken and serve immediately. *(Makes 6 servings.)*

French Salad

> Endive, romaine, other kinds of lettuce, and leeks with green tops
> 2 tablespoons wine vinegar
> 6 tablespoons salad oil
> ½ teaspoon salt
> ¼ teaspoon coarsely ground black pepper
> 1 clove garlic, mashed or chopped into bits
> Tiny bread cubes

Tear greens and toss with vinegar, oil, and seasonings. Fry bread cubes in bacon fat with a little garlic until cubes are browned. Drain on paper, then put on top of tossed salad.

The Long French Loaf

1 cake or envelope yeast

1½ cups lukewarm water

1½ teaspoons salt

5 cups sifted plain flour

Soften yeast in ¼ cup lukewarm water. When yeast is soft, stir in salt and 1¼ cups lukewarm water. Mix well. Gradually mix in about 5 cups flour, or enough to make a dough that pulls away from sides of bowl with just a little stickiness.

Turn dough out onto a lightly floured board and knead until it becomes elastic and smooth. Place dough in a buttered bowl, cover with a clean towel, and put in a warm place to rise for about 2 hours. It should double in bulk in that time.

Punch dough down and let rise again for about 45 minutes, or until again double in bulk. Turn it out on a floured board and knead it for a minute or two. Divide dough in half and form each half into a long roll.

Place loaves on a buttered baking sheet and let rise in a warm place until twice their original size. Cut small diagonal slits ¼-inch deep across top of loaves when they are half risen. Brush surface with a little milk and bake in a hot oven (400 degrees) until loaves are golden brown.

Tutti-Frutti Flambée

½ cup sliced fresh strawberries

½ cup peeled and sliced fresh peaches

½ cup sliced bananas

½ cup canned crushed pineapple, drained

½ cup chopped preserved figs

½ cup canned mandarin orange segments

2 tablespoons sugar

½ cup Cointreau or other orange-flavored liqueur

1 cup cognac

Mix fruits with sugar and Cointreau. Let stand covered in a cool place for at least 1 hour.

When ready to serve, remove to a chafing dish or serving dish. Heat cognac very hot, ignite, and pour over fruit. Serve flaming fruit quickly over ice cream. *(Makes 6 servings.)*

Frank'n'Stein Party

LAGER BEER CUP

GIGGLE-GAGGLE
HALF-AND-HALF, AMERICAN STYLE
'ALF-AND-'ALF, ENGLISH STYLE
STUFFED FRANKFURTERS
ROLLMOP POTATO SALAD
KRAUT
PRETZELS
FLADEN MIT SPINAT

SACHER TORTE

Lager Beer Cup

Rind of 1 lemon	**1 tablespoon sugar**
½ cup water	**Few mint leaves, fresh or dried**
1 cup dry sherry	**Pinch of grated nutmeg**
Juice of 2 lemons	**1 pint lager beer or any good ale**

Remove lemon rind in thin fine strips, put them in a jug, add water, sherry, lemon juice, sugar, mint, and nutmeg. Cover and let liquid stand for 1 hour. Strain into pitcher; add a few pieces of ice and beer or ale. Serve in steins. *(Makes 2 steins.)*

Giggle-Gaggle

Good ale	**Bourbon**
Ginger beer	

Pour equal quantities of ale and ginger beer into a pitcher with some ice cubes. Add a dash of bourbon and, when quite cold, serve in steins.

Half-and-Half, American Style

Fill glass half full of beer and fill up with porter.

'Alf-and-'Alf, English Style

Fill stein half full of beer and fill up with ale.

Stuffed Frankfurters

1½ cups uncooked elbow, shell, or small macaroni
¾ cup evaporated milk
1¼ teaspoons dry mustard
1¼ teaspoons salt
⅛ teaspoon pepper
2½ cups grated American cheese
1½ pounds frankfurters

Cook macaroni in boiling salted water until tender. Drain. Combine milk, mustard, salt, pepper, and 2 cups of cheese in a double boiler, and cook until cheese is melted and sauce is smooth, stirring constantly. Add macaroni and mix well. Split large frankfurters lengthwise without separating them entirely and fill with macaroni mixture. Sprinkle with remaining cheese, and bake at 400 degrees for 15 minutes. Serve at once. *(Makes 6 servings.)*

Rollmop Potato Salad

4 large potatoes
2 tablespoons olive oil
1 tablespoon wine vinegar
6 rollmops (herring fillets, pickled and rolled in sour cream)
½ cup chopped gherkins
½ cup chopped parsley
½ teaspoon salt
¼ teaspoon coarsely ground black pepper
Sour cream

Boil potatoes in their skins, peel, and slice while still warm. Toss potato slices with olive oil and vinegar. Chop rollmops and gherkins. Add them to potatoes. Add parsley, salt, and pepper. Taste for correct amount of seasoning. Add enough sour cream to mix salad well and chill before serving. *(Makes 6 servings.)*

Kraut

4 cups sauerkraut	¾ teaspoon salt
3 cups sour cream	⅓ cup bacon drippings
3 medium-sized raw potatoes, peeled and grated	2 medium onions, grated
⅓ teaspoon coarsely ground black pepper	1 teaspoon caraway seeds
	½ teaspoon ground cloves
	2 bay leaves

Drain sauerkraut and place in kettle with sour cream for 45 minutes over low heat. Add other ingredients and simmer for 45 minutes longer. *(Makes 6 servings.)*

Pretzels

¼ cup (½ stick) butter	Salt
1¾ cups flour	Pepper
2 egg whites, beaten	Milk
2 egg yolks, beaten	Coarse salt

Cream butter and work into flour with egg whites and yolks, a little salt and pepper. Roll out on a floured board. To shape dough into figures eight, brush with milk, cut strips, and roll. Sprinkle with coarse salt. Bake in a moderately hot oven for 10 minutes. *(Makes 12 fairly large pretzels.)*

Fladen Mit Spinat

2 tablespoons butter	Salt
1 small onion, finely chopped	Pepper
2 cups spinach puree (use baby food)	Thin pancakes
1 tablespoon cream	3 eggs
1 tablespoon flour	2 cups milk

Melt butter and fry onion lightly. Add spinach puree and cream. Sprinkle in flour. Season with salt and pepper to taste, and stir over heat a few minutes. Have ready some thin pancakes. Spread each one with spinach mixture. Roll them up and place in a baking dish or deep pie dish. Beat eggs well, stir in milk, add salt and pepper to taste, and pour over pancakes. Bake at 350 degrees until custard is set, then serve. *(Makes 6 servings.)*

Sacher Torte

This is the Old House version of the famous chocolate tart made at the venerable Sacher Hotel in Vienna.

CAKE:

½ pound bar bitter chocolate
Water
½ pound (2 sticks) butter
8 eggs, separated, yolks and
  whites beaten

8 ounces ground almonds
¾ cup sugar
1 tablespoon cornstarch

Melt chocolate with a little water. Cream butter, chocolate, egg yolks, almonds, and sugar. Beat till light and creamy. Add cornstarch and beat again.

Fold in stiffly beaten egg whites. Spoon gently into buttered cake tin dusted with flour and sugar. Bake at 300 degrees for 1 hour. Cool thoroughly in tin, then turn out.

FILLING:

4 egg yolks
2 tablespoons sugar
2 tablespoons cocoa
½ cup thick or double cream
1 tablespoon sugar mixed with
  1 teaspoon vanilla

1 cup apricot jam
1 cup chocolate frosting (made
  from mix or your favorite
  recipe)

Cook egg yolks, sugar, and cocoa in top of a double boiler, stirring constantly until thickened. Allow to cool. Whip cream and add sugar-vanilla mixture, and fold into cooled cocoa mixture.

Cut cake into two layers and spread filling thickly on bottom layer. Replace top and spread apricot jam over. Spread chocolate frosting over jam, and serve this glorious dessert with whipped cream on the side. (*Cake can be cut into 6 large portions.*)

After=Five=Hostess Dinner Party

WILD-EYED ROSE HIGHBALL

WIDOW'S KISS

KING CRAB MEAT
A LA OLD HOUSE

RICE SUPREME

BRUSSELS SPROUTS
IN PAPER BAGS

CHEDDAR CHEESE MOLDED SALAD

BRANDIED GINGERBREAD
WITH BRANDY SAUCE

AFTER-DINNER COFFEE FRAPPE

❋ *After-Five-Hostess Dinner Party*

For working women who have to organize their time, here is a dinner that may be entirely prepared days or hours before, and simply reheated in the oven before serving. If tastefully arranged and served buffet style, it will bring forth much admiration. Single working women, note: This dinner is a fine one to serve to any male upon whom you have designs.

Wild-Eyed Rose Highball

Juice of ½ lime	**2 ounces Irish whiskey**
½ ounce grenadine	**Club soda**

Put lime juice, grenadine, and whiskey in 8-ounce highball glass, add an ice cube, fill glass with club soda, and stir gently.

Widow's Kiss

½ ounce yellow chartreuse 1 ounce apple brandy
½ ounce Benedictine 1 dash bitters

Shake with cracked ice and strain into cocktail glass. A fresh strawberry should be served on top.

King Crabmeat à la Old House

5 egg yolks
1 tablespoon water
1 pound (2 cups) melted butter, just lukewarm
1 tablespoon lemon juice
3 level tablespoons dry mustard
1 teaspoon salt
½ teaspoon pepper
¼ cup A-1 Sauce
Thyme
5-pound package frozen cooked king crabmeat, thawed
2 tablespoons chopped parsley

In a double boiler, put egg yolks, beaten lightly with water. Little by little add melted butter, stirring briskly. When sauce has thickened, take it from heat and beat or stir very fast, adding lemon juice, dry mustard, salt, and pepper. Stir in A-1 Sauce and add a pinch of thyme. Sauce will take on a slightly curdled look.

Remove from heat and use immediately, or keep in the refrigerator and reheat when needed. Mix thoroughly with crabmeat. Stir in parsley and serve over Rice Supreme. *(Makes 6 servings.)*

Rice Supreme

Cook 1 package Near East (or any East Indian) rice pilaf as per instructions on package. After rice is cooked and stirred lightly, mix in 2 tablespoons chopped parsley, 2 tablespoons dehydrated minced onions, and 2 tablespoons finely chopped almonds, cashews, or walnuts. *(Makes 6 servings.)*

Brussels Sprouts in Paper Bags

Paper-bag cookery has been known since the seventeenth century. The use of bags aids in the retention of juices and flavorings. The process is simple. Today grocers have parchment sandwich bags that are just the right size for an individual serving. The bags must be well buttered inside and out before the food is placed in them.

Use frozen brussels sprouts, as these cook much quicker than fresh ones and are easier to prepare. Be sure that they are well thawed first, and well drained.

Fill buttered bags with brussels sprouts, a little over half full. Sprinkle sprouts with salt, pepper, and ground dill, and add ½ teaspoon butter. Fold open ends over several times and seal with paper clips. Place bags on a baking sheet and put them in a preheated slow oven at 200 degrees. Cook brussels sprouts in their bags for 1 hour. Remove clips and serve the bags on a fluffy bed of parsley on a tray.

Cheddar Cheese Molded Salad

1 envelope unflavored gelatin
1 tablespoon sugar
1 teaspoon celery salt
½ cup water
2 cups concentrated cheddar
  cheese soup, undiluted
2 tablespoons horseradish

1 cup finely diced green pepper
1 cup chopped onions
1 cup canned button
  mushrooms, drained
¼ teaspoon coarsely ground
  black pepper

Mix gelatin, sugar, and salt. Add warm water and stir until gelatin is dissolved. Blend cheese soup and gelatin mixture together. Fold in remaining ingredients and mix well. Turn into 5-cup mold or individual molds and chill until firm. Unmold on serving plate and garnish with salad greens and radish roses. *(Makes 6 servings.)*

Brandied Gingerbread

½ cup bacon drippings
1 cup brown sugar, firmly
  packed
2 eggs
1 teaspoon grated lemon rind
2 cups sifted flour
1 teaspoon nutmeg

1 teaspoon baking soda
½ teaspoon salt
½ teaspoon powdered ginger
½ cup boiling water
½ cup dark molasses (sorghum,
  if obtainable)
2 tablespoons good brandy

Cream bacon drippings and sugar together. Beat in eggs one at a time. Add grated rind. Sift flour with nutmeg, soda, salt, and ginger.

Combine boiling water and molasses in a bowl. Add sifted and liquid ingredients alternately to first mixture. Beat well after each addition. Blend in brandy last. Pour into a greased, lightly floured pan and bake at 350 degrees for 40 minutes. Serve with Brandy Sauce. *(Makes 6 to 8 servings.)*

Brandy Sauce
Men love this sauce!

1 tablespoon butter	1 cup hot water
2 cups brown sugar	½ cup brandy
1 heaping tablespoon flour	

Cream butter, sugar, and flour together. Add water a little at a time. Cook in double boiler or over water until thick. Cool to warm and add brandy.

After-Dinner Coffee Frappe

2 ounces Tia Maria	1 ounce Cointreau

Fill roly-poly or Old-Fashioned glass half full of shaved ice and pour Tia Maria and Cointreau over, stirring slightly.

Dinner Party for Dieters

BRANDY COCKTAIL
ANISETTE COCKTAIL
MERRY WIDOW FIZZ

COTTAGE CHEESE DIP
FOR RAW VEGETABLES
CHOWHOUND CHICKEN
HEAD LETTUCE WITH ROQUEFORT DRESSING
BAKED HERBED POTATOES

CHOCOLATE PIE

Brandy Cocktail

2 ounces brandy	2 dashes bitters
3 drops liquid sugar substitute	Twist of lemon peel

Stir with cracked ice and strain into 3-ounce cocktail glass. *(70 calories)*

Anisette Cocktail

1½ ounces anisette	1 dash orange bitters
3 drops liquid sugar substitute	1 ounce water

Shake with cracked ice and strain into 3-ounce cocktail glass. *(80 calories)*

Merry Widow Fizz

Juice of ½ orange	1 egg white
Juice of ½ lemon	1½ ounces sloe gin
⅛ teaspoon liquid sugar substitute	Club soda, chilled

Shake all ingredients but soda with cracked ice and strain into 8-ounce highball glass. Fill with cold soda. *(70 calories)*

Cottage Cheese Dip

¼ cup buttermilk
1 cup cottage cheese
¼ teaspoon lemon juice
⅛ teaspoon coarsely ground
    black pepper

⅛ teaspoon salt
1 tablespoon minced fresh onion
1 teaspoon paprika
⅛ teaspoon chili powder

Beat until thick and creamy, preferably in a blender. *(Makes 1 cup; 15 calories per tablespoon.)*

Serve with raw carrot curls, celery sticks, cauliflowerettes, cherry tomatoes, radishes, cucumber fingers.

Chowhound Chicken

6 chicken drumsticks and
    6 breasts
1 tablespoon margarine
1 clove garlic, minced
1 cup minced onion
1 cup minced celery
½ cup minced green pepper

1-pound can (2 cups) tomatoes,
    chopped
1 teaspoon salt
¼ teaspoon thyme
1 bay leaf
⅛ teaspoon coarsely ground
    black pepper

Saute chicken drumsticks and breasts in the margarine over a low heat, turning frequently, until browned. Add all other ingredients and mix well. Cover chicken tightly, and cook over low heat until chicken is tender and juice from tomatoes is absorbed. A little extra tomato juice may be added if necessary. *(Makes 6 servings; 150 calories per serving.)*

Head Lettuce with Roquefort Dressing

Small head of lettuce
4 tablespoons tarragon vinegar
1 clove garlic, pressed and
    chopped to bits
½ teaspoon paprika
½ teaspoon salt

½ teaspoon liquid sugar
    substitute
2 tablespoons crumbled
    Roquefort or blue cheese
1 tablespoon chopped onion
1 tablespoon dried parsley flakes

Divide lettuce head into 6 wedges. Mix all remaining ingredients well and serve over lettuce wedges. *(Makes 6 servings; 25 calories per serving.)*

Baked Herbed Potatoes

6 medium-sized Idaho potatoes	1 teaspoon salt
¾ cup hot skim milk	1 tablespoon chopped chervil
1 tablespoon grated onion	1 teaspoon paprika
⅛ teaspoon coarsely ground black pepper	2 tablespoons grated Parmesan cheese

Wash potatoes thoroughly, and while wet wrap in foil and bake for 1 hour, or until potatoes are soft when squeezed. Cut a thin slice from flat side of each potato and scoop out shell. Mix potato with other ingredients except cheese, and beat until light and fluffy. Pile herbed potato mixture back into shells and sprinkle with cheese. Put back into oven until potatoes are slightly browned on top. *(Makes 6 servings; 60 calories per serving.)*

Chocolate Pie

Split 8 ladyfingers and use to line an 8-inch pie pan. Blend 3 envelopes D-Zerta chocolate dietary pudding with 2½ cups skim milk. Bring to a boil, stirring constantly. Cool 15 minutes. Stir and spoon into pie pan. Dot top while soft with miniature marshmallows. Chill in refrigerator until firm. Cut pie into 6 wedges. *(87 calories per wedge.)*

The Twelve Most Popular
Mixed Drinks at The Old House

Dry Martini

1½ ounces dry gin
⅛ ounce dry vermouth —
   a dash!

Dash of orange bitters

Put in mixing glass with cracked ice and stir well. Strain into cocktail glass and drop in an olive, a tomolive, or a pickled cocktail eggplant.

Manhattan

¾ ounce sweet vermouth
1½ ounces bourbon whiskey

Dash of bitters

Stir well in mixing glass with a few pieces of cracked ice. Strain into cocktail glass and drop in a cherry.

Tom Collins

Squeeze the juice of ½ lemon over 1 teaspoon confectioners' sugar. Add 2 ounces dry gin and several ice cubes. Fill glass with club soda and stir well. Drop in a cherry and a slice of lemon. Cut a slice of orange in half and place over brim of glass. Serve with a straw.

Daiquiri

For each serving, use the juice of 1 lime, 1 teaspoon confectioners' sugar, and 1½ ounces light rum. Shake well with a few pieces of cracked ice in cocktail shaker and strain into cocktail glass.

Old-Fashioned

Muddle ½ teaspoon sugar with 2 dashes angostura bitters and enough water to cover in Old-Fashioned glass. Add an ice cube and 2 ounces bourbon whiskey and stir well. Twist a piece of lemon rind and drop in; add a slice of orange and a cherry. Serve with a stirring rod. An elegant touch is a stirrer coated with a big lump of rock candy, which can be purchased at most gourmet shops.

Whiskey Sour

Juice of ½ lemon   2 ounces bourbon whiskey
½ teaspoon confectioners' sugar Club soda

Shake lemon juice, sugar, and bourbon well with cracked ice and strain into 6-ounce glass. Fill glass with soda. Decorate with ½ slice of lemon and a cherry.

Screwdriver

Put 2 or 3 ice cubes into 6-ounce glass. Add 2 ounces vodka. Fill balance of glass with orange juice and stir.

Rob Roy

¾ ounce sweet vermouth   Dash of orange bitters
1½ ounces Scotch whiskey

Stir well with cracked ice and strain into cocktail glass.

Planter's Punch

Juice of 1 lime   2 ounces dark rum
Juice of ½ lemon   1 ounce Jamaica rum
Juice of ½ orange   ¼ teaspoon curaçao
1 teaspoon pineapple juice

Pour fruit juices and dark rum into large glass, well filled with shaved ice. Stir until glass is frosted. Then add Jamaica rum and top with curaçao. Decorate with slices of orange, lemon, and pineapple, a cherry, also a sprig of mint dipped in confectioners' sugar. Serve with a straw.

Cuba Libre

Squeeze ½ lime and drop it with the juice into highball glass. Add 2 ounces dark rum and 2 ice cubes. Fill glass with cola and stir.

Rum Collins

Put juice of 1 lime, 1 teaspoon confectioners' sugar, and 2 ounces light rum with several ice cubes in highball glass. Fill glass with club soda and stir well. Place a slice of lemon on the brim, drop in a cherry and squeezed lime, and serve with a straw.

Champagne Cocktail

2 dashes angostura bitters	Champagne
1 lump sugar	Spiral rind of ½ lemon

Use 6-ounce champagne glass. Put bitters on sugar in bottom of glass. Fill glass with champagne. Drop in lemon rind.

Index